FLOYD CLYMER'S MOTORCYCLIST'S LIBRARY

The Book of the
VILLIERS ENGINE

THE RUNNING AND MAINTENANCE OF VILLIERS ENGINES (MODELS UP TO 1959) WITH A CHAPTER ON THE BOND MINICAR, THE A.C. "PETITE," AND THE GORDON

BY
CYRIL GRANGE

*1958 Tenth edition
Includes 1959 Supplement
from the Eleventh edition*

ANNOUNCEMENT

By special arrangement with the original publishers of this book, Sir Isaac Pitman & Son, Ltd., of London, England, we have secured the exclusive publishing rights for this book, as well as all others in THE MOTORCYCLIST'S LIBRARY.

Included in THE MOTORCYCLIST'S LIBRARY are complete instruction manuals covering the care and operation of respective motorcycles and engines; valuable data on speed tuning, and thrilling accounts of motorcycle race events. See listing of available titles elsewhere in this edition.

We consider it a privilege to be able to offer so many fine titles to our customers.

FLOYD CLYMER
Publisher of Books Pertaining to Automobiles and Motorcycles
2125 W. PICO ST.   LOS ANGELES 6, CALIF.

INTRODUCTION

Welcome to the world of digital publishing ~ the book you now hold in your hand, while unchanged from the original edition, was printed using the latest state of the art digital technology. The advent of print-on-demand has forever changed the publishing process, never has information been so accessible and it is our hope that this book serves your informational needs for years to come. If this is your first exposure to digital publishing, we hope that you are pleased with the results. Many more titles of interest to the classic automobile and motorcycle enthusiast, collector and restorer are available via our website at www.VelocePress.com. We hope that you find this title as interesting as we do.

NOTE FROM THE PUBLISHER

The information presented is true and complete to the best of our knowledge. All recommendations are made without any guarantees on the part of the author or the publisher, who also disclaim all liability incurred with the use of this information.

TRADEMARKS

We recognize that some words, model names and designations, for example, mentioned herein are the property of the trademark holder. We use them for identification purposes only. This is not an official publication.

INFORMATION ON THE USE OF THIS PUBLICATION

This manual is an invaluable resource for the classic motorcycle enthusiast and a "must have" for owners interested in performing their own maintenance. However, in today's information age we are constantly subject to changes in common practice, new technology, availability of improved materials and increased awareness of chemical toxicity. As such, it is advised that the user consult with an experienced professional prior to undertaking any procedure described herein. While every care has been taken to ensure correctness of information, it is obviously not possible to guarantee complete freedom from errors or omissions or to accept liability arising from such errors or omissions. Therefore, any individual that uses the information contained within, or elects to perform or participate in do-it-yourself repairs or modifications acknowledges that there is a risk factor involved and that the publisher or its associates cannot be held responsible for personal injury or property damage resulting from the use of the information or the outcome of such procedures.

WARNING!

One final word of advice, this publication is intended to be used as a reference guide, and when in doubt the reader should consult with a qualified technician.

PREFACE

THIS handbook has been written by a practical motor-cyclist who has had long and delightful experience with various Villiers engined motor-cycles. In September, 1956, the two-millionth Villiers engine left the assembly lines, machines remarkable for their economy, freedom from trouble, for their low cost, and for utility purposes.

There is now a very large number of firms who install this proprietary engine in their motor-cycles. Realizing this fact, and desiring in the limited space available to present as much useful information as possible, the author has thought it best to omit all reference to the overhauling of the actual machines as distinct from the engines. The engine, after all, is *the* important thing in a motor-cycle, and that which requires the most attention—attention which is well rewarded.

On the following pages the reader will find all the information he requires on the handling, maintenance, and overhauling of these little Villiers two-stroke engines.

In Chapter I the principle of the two-stroke engine is fully described, and the special features of the Villiers engines enumerated. Thereafter follows a chapter giving full details of the various power units now marketed.

Chapter V is the longest chapter, and the author has done his best to present to the reader all information necessary for overhauling and dismantling. Special chapters are devoted to the subjects of Carburation and Ignition, the principles as well as the Villiers system being dealt with.

Chapter IX is devoted to the application of the Villiers engine to the light car.

The author would, in conclusion, express his appreciation of the courtesy shown by the Villiers Engineering Company, Ltd., Wolverhampton, in supplying information and photographs which have very materially assisted in the compilation of this book.

SPECIAL NOTE

In addition to motor-cycles and auto-cycles, there are many thousands of Villiers engines used for agricultural and stationary purposes.

The majority of motor lawn mowers made in Great Britain are fitted with Villiers two-stroke engines, which are also employed for propelling light aeroplanes, motor rollers, railway trollies, farm cultivators, delivery vans, invalid chairs, and for driving compressors, pumps, house lighting sets, saws, etc. Various types of engines are employed for the different purposes, and although some of them are fitted with specially designed fans and cowling for cooling purposes, the following particulars in this book will apply to all of them in general, and, if the instructions are followed, will enable the best results to be obtained from these units.

Complete details of these installations are at all times available from the manufacturers.

CONTENTS

CHAP		PAGE
	Preface	
I.	How the Two-stroke Engine Works	1
II.	Types of Villiers Two-stroke Motor-cycle Engines	7
III.	Lubrication	32
IV.	How to Handle the Villiers Engine	38
V.	Overhauling	46
VI.	The Villiers Fly-wheel Magneto	65
VII.	The Villiers Carburettor	77
VIII.	The Villiers Electric Lighting Systems	92
IX.	Three-wheeled Cars	106
	Appendix A 1959 Villiers Engine Supplement	115
	Appendix B	121
	Index	123

CHAPTER I

HOW THE TWO-STROKE ENGINE WORKS

IN the opening and introductory chapter of this book we will, for the benefit of those readers of small technical knowledge and at the risk of boring the more advanced student of motor-cycling matters, outline briefly the principle on which the two-stroke engine works, and in succeeding chapters we will deal with the care, maintenance, and running of the Villiers motor-cycle engines, all of which are of two-stroke design. Before considering the actual cycle of operations, it is necessary first to reflect upon the construction of the two-stroke engine.

The Working Parts. The two-stroke engine is vastly simpler than the four-stroke type; there is no complicated valve mechanism needing constant adjustment and overhauling. Therein lies the beauty of the two-stroke. Simplicity is the key-note throughout. For utility purposes, and for the rider who has no time for constantly working on his engine, the two-stroke engine has no equal. Moreover, the two-stroke is well known to possess a degree of reliability as yet unattained by other types of power units.

Fig. 1 illustrates the moving parts of a two-stroke engine, and it will be noticed that they are three in number; the PISTON, the CONNECTING ROD, and the CRANKSHAFT ASSEMBLY. Let us deal with them in this order.

The Piston. This is a cylindrical body of cast iron or aluminium alloy fitted with spring rings which enable a gas-tight fit to be constantly maintained between the piston and the walls of the cylinder in which it reciprocates. A pin known as the gudgeon pin passes through the diametrical centre, and forms the axis for the *small-end* bearing of the connecting rod. The top of the piston on pre-war models is shaped to *form a deflector*, the duty of which will be understood upon referring to the cycle of operations explained later.

From 1934 onwards modern design has led to the use of more efficient engines with flat-top pistons.

The Connecting Rod. The connecting rod is a stiff " H " section rod connecting the piston to the crankshaft, the duty of which is to transmit the downward thrust of the piston to the crankshaft, thereby converting reciprocating into rotary movement. Its lower end reciprocates on the crank pin, and this is known as the big-end bearing.

The Crankshaft Assembly. This comprises the crank pin with nuts, the cranks with their projecting shafts, and the balance weights. This crankshaft is carried by means of bearings in each side of the crankcase, in which the shaft rotates. Mounted on the crankshaft outside the crankcase is a heavy-rimmed fly-wheel, which stores up energy and helps the engine to run evenly, at the same time enabling it to maintain its revolutions when the power impulses have ceased.

All other parts of the engine are stationary, such as the carburettor, which supplies a combustible mixture, the magneto which generates a spark at the plug points and causes the combustible charge to be fired. These two components are described in separate chapters later.

Bolted on to the crankcase is the cylinder in which are ports for the entry and exit of the gases.

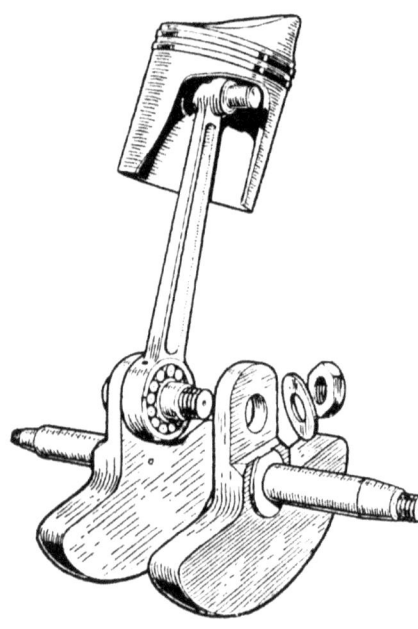

Fig. 1. The Moving Parts of a Two-stroke Engine

An internal combustion engine derives its power from gases which are forced into the cylinder, where they are ignited, and the consequent pressure developed forces down the piston which, in turn, rotates the crankshaft. This cycle of operations is achieved in the simplest manner in a two-stroke engine. There are types of internal combustion engines requiring valves with complicated operating mechanisms, or, in some instances, special sleeves which have to describe involved rotating and reciprocating movements, but in the two-stroke engine the piston itself is arranged to cover all these duties, thus enabling the minimum of parts to be employed to give the same results. Apart from its simplicity, the two-stroke engine has a big advantage in giving a power impulse for every revolution, whereas other types of engines only give a power impulse for two revolutions. It will be understood, therefore, that the torque, which means the power thrust, is much more even and, in the two-stroke, has no harshness.

HOW THE TWO-STROKE ENGINE WORKS

Let us now study the actual cycle of operations which is made clear by the following description and reference to Fig. 2A.

The Two-stroke Cycle. It is important that the crankcase of a two-stroke engine should be perfectly gas-tight, because this compartment acts as a compression chamber. The piston itself compresses the gases at the top and the underside of its head. The diagrams, of the three-port engine with the deflector-type piston Fig. 2A, show clearly the various ports in the cylinder. The carburettor which supplies the mixture to the engine is attached to the *inlet port*, whilst the *transfer port* is a connecting passage between the crankcase and the cylinder barrel. The *exhaust port* is, of course, the final exit for the burned gases.

Assume, first of all, that the piston is at the bottom of its stroke and is about to ascend, thus creating suction in the crankcase; on ascending the piston will uncover the inlet port from the carburettor, as shown in Fig. 2A (2), allowing fresh gases to enter the crankcase. Meanwhile, in the combustion chamber the burned gases from a previous combustion have been driven out through the exhaust port and the piston is compressing a fresh charge (Fig. 2A (3)). When the gases are compressed in the cylinder head, a spark occurs at the sparking plug igniting these gases, causing a combustion which forces the piston on its next downward stroke, and in descending it compresses the gases which have been collected in the crankcase, and the top of the piston first uncovers the exhaust port, allowing the burned gases to pass from the combustion chamber, and then a little farther down its stroke uncovers the transfer port. The compressed gases in the crankcase then force their way through the transfer port, and are directed by means of the deflector of the piston head upwards into the combustion chamber (Fig. 2A (1)). The object of the deflector on the piston is now apparent. If the piston had a flat top the gases from the transfer port would shoot straight across, and a big proportion would be lost through the exhaust port. The deflector therefore projects the gases upwards, and they actually help to push out burned gases. Thus the cycle of operations is continued, the gases being drawn from the carburettor, compressed in the crankcase, transferred to the cylinder head, then ignited and expelled.

It will be seen that the functioning of a two-stroke engine, therefore, is exceedingly simple, and, probably most important of all, there are no delicate parts to get out of order. The absence of gear wheels and tappets for valve operating mechanism also makes the two-stroke engine quiet mechanically.

The cycle of operations of the more modern two-stroke engine which is equipped with a flat-topped piston, is shown in Fig. 2B.

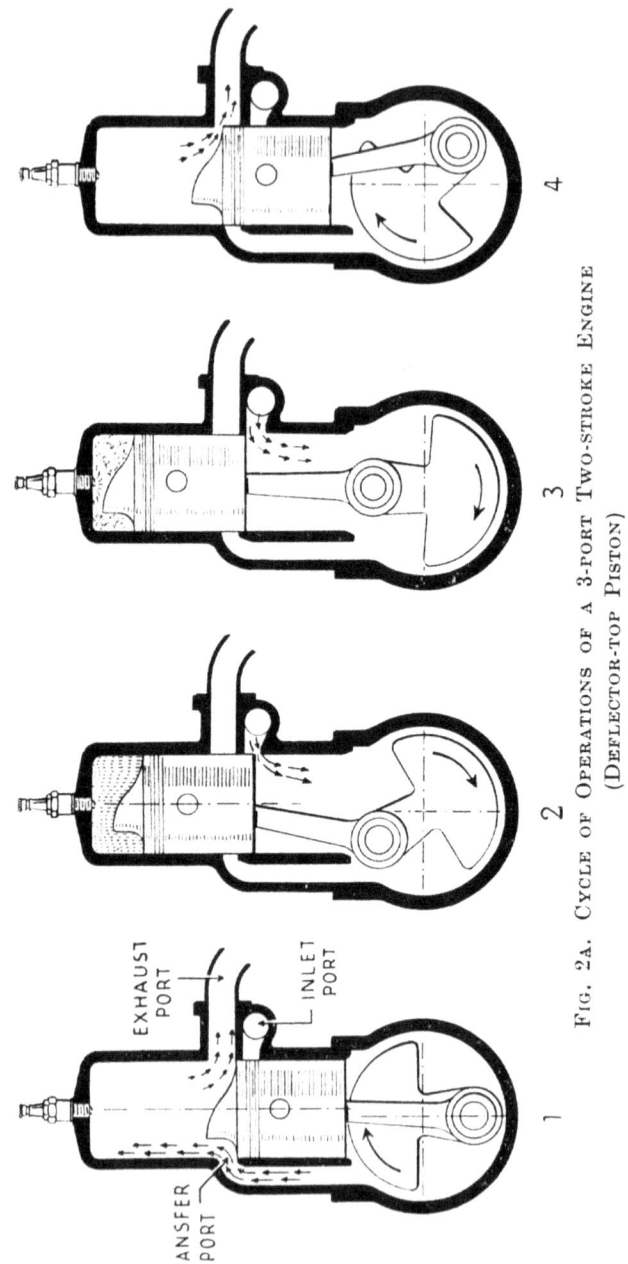

Fig. 2a. Cycle of Operations of a 3-port Two-stroke Engine (Deflector-top Piston)

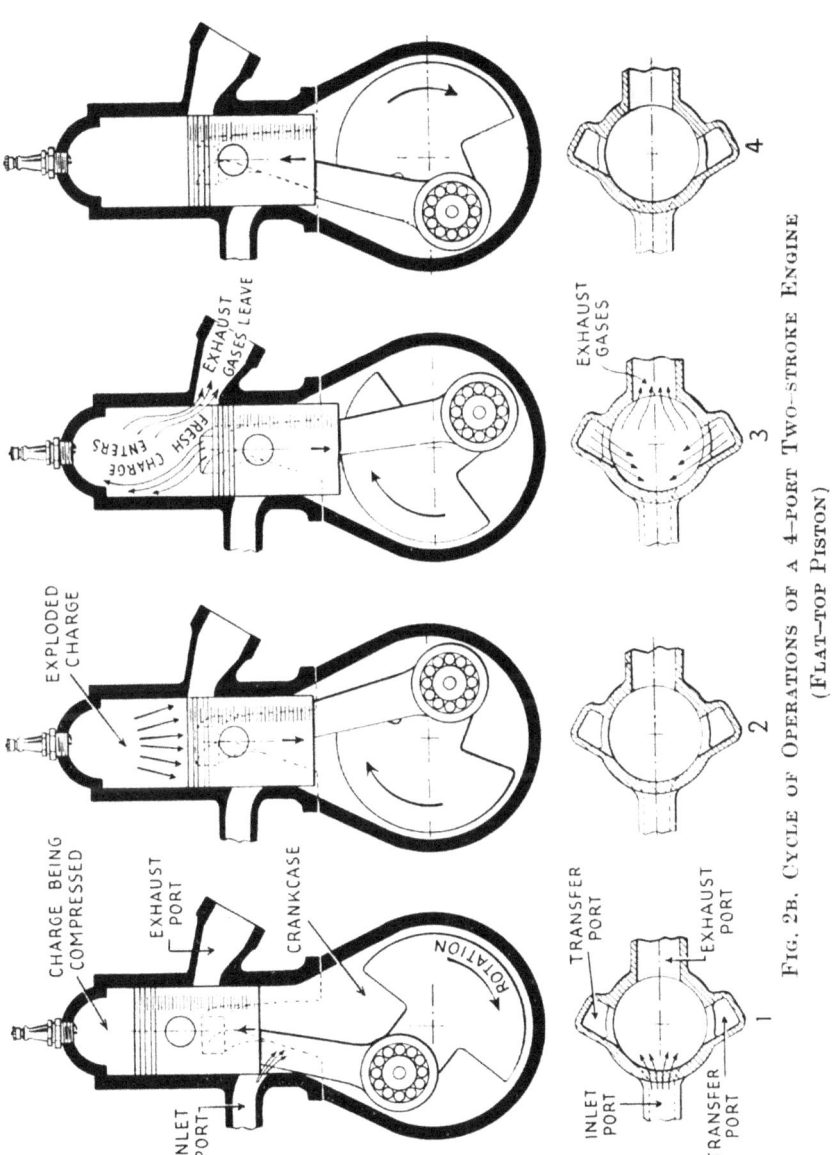

Fig. 2b. Cycle of Operations of a 4-port Two-stroke Engine (Flat-top Piston)

In the first part of the cycle, on the upstroke of the piston (Fig. 2B (1)), a partial vacuum is created in the crankcase. The piston skirt uncovers the inlet port and a mixture of petroil and air is drawn into the crankcase from the carburettor. The previous charge of petroil and air is compressed in the combustion chamber by the upward movement of the piston and fired, causing the piston to descend and compress the mixture in the crankcase, Fig. 2B (2). Near the bottom of the stroke the top edge of the piston uncovers the exhaust and transfer ports, Fig. 2B (3). The burnt gases escape and a fresh charge enters the cylinder through the transfer ports. The piston then starts a new cycle, Fig. 2B (4), which is shown again in Fig. 2B (1). A more detailed explanation of the flow of gases is given on page 22.

CHAPTER II

TYPES OF VILLIERS TWO-STROKE MOTOR-CYCLE ENGINES

THE Villiers Engineering Co., Ltd., market various different sizes and types of engines ranging from 50 c.c. ($\frac{1}{2}$ h.p.) to 353 c.c. ($3\frac{1}{2}$ h.p.). Here it might be as well to point out that c.c. means " cubic centimetres," and represents the actual volume of the cylinder swept by the piston. As a convenient formula, 100 c.c. is taken to represent 1 h.p., so that it will be seen that the small 147 c.c. engine is really 1·47 h.p., or 1$\frac{1}{2}$ h.p.

Actually, the power developed by each of the engines is considerably more than the nominal figure obtained by this formula, which, however, is a convenient method of describing them. The range of Villiers engines covers all needs, and includes models for low priced utility motor-cycles; for sports machines, and for lightweight sidecar combinations.

A number of British motor-cycle manufacturers fit Villiers engines in their machines as standard. Most of these motor-cycles are quite suitable for long distance touring which calls for hard-wearing qualities.

In this chapter, we describe the principal features of the various engines, and set forth specifications of each model including those which are no longer being manufactured.

Current productions include the Mark 2 F, 98 c.c. auto-cycle engine; the Mark 4 F, 98 c.c. 2-speed unit; the Mark 30 C, 147 c.c. 3-speed unit; the Mark 29 C, competition model of 30 C; the Mark 29 C/4, as Mark 29 C but with a 4-speed gear-box; the Mark 8 E, 197 c.c. 3-speed unit; the Mark 8 E/4, as Mark 8 E but with a 4-speed gear-box; the Mark 8 E/R 3-speed unit with reverse and fan cooling; the Mark 7 E, the competition model of 8 E; the Mark 7 E/4, as Mark 7 E but with a 4-speed gear-box and the Mark 1 H, the 225 c.c. 4-speed unit; also the Mark 28 B, 353 c.c. 3-speed and reverse unit, fan-cooled for light cars. See also Appendix.

Engine Specifications. All Villiers engines are of the single-cylinder type. Each model is distinguished by its name or mark number cast on the outside of the transfer port on the cylinder, and every engine has a number with one or more letters prefixed stamped on the sprocket side of the crankcase immediately below the cylinder flange. Each type of engine has a different prefixed letter (or letters), so that by quoting these letters and

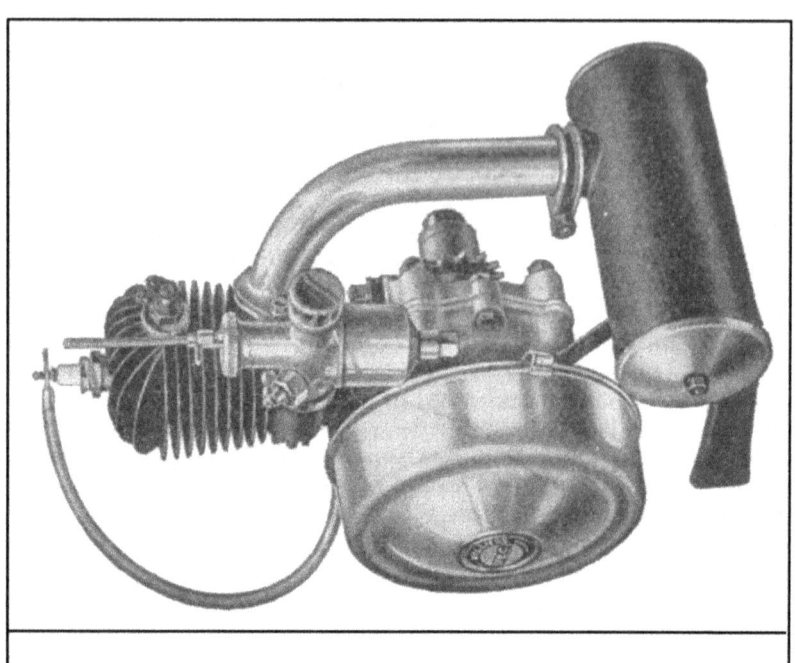

Fig. 4. The 147 c.c. Engine

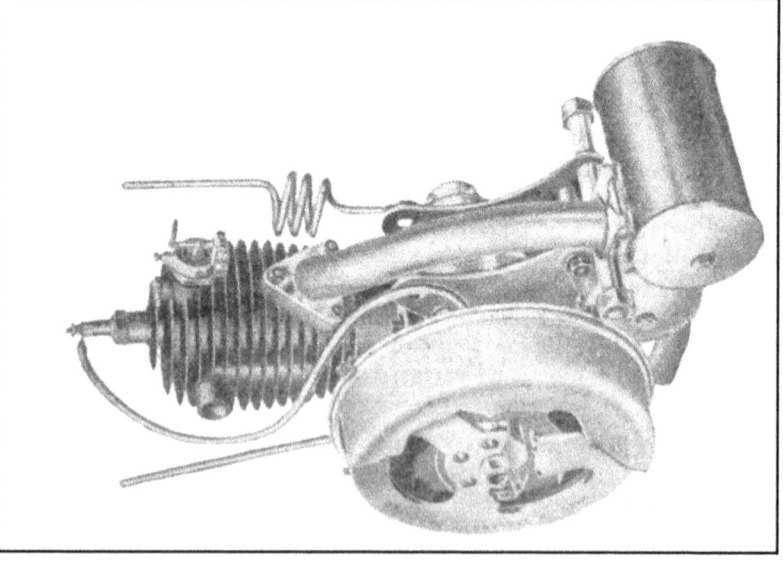

Fig. 3. The 249 c.c. Mark V (1922) Engine

TYPES OF VILLIERS TWO-STROKE ENGINES

numbers together, the manufacturers know the exact pattern of engine referred to. The tax on a machine fitted with the 50 c.c., 98 c.c., 147 c.c. or the 148 c.c. engine is 17s. 6d., regardless of weight; from 150–250 c.c., £1 17s. 6d.; exceeding 250 c.c., £3 15s.; for a sidecar under 250 c.c., £3 2s. 6d.; exceeding 250 c.c., £5 per annum.

Mark I to V Models. These were the first two-stroke types

FIG. 5. THE 98 C.C. "JUNIOR" DE-LUXE ENGINE

manufactured by the Villiers Engineering Co., Ltd., and are distinguished by the flat fins on the cylinder head. (All models subsequent to the Mark V pattern have the fins of the cylinder running across the head.) The cubic capacity of these engines is 269 c.c., and each has a bore of 70 mm. and a stroke of 70 mm. The pistons and cylinders are all of cast iron and the gudgeon pins are a "driving fit" in the pistons, and not fully floating.

The crankshaft bearings and the small-end are long phosphor-bronze bushes, whilst the big-end is a roller bearing. Mark I, II, and III, and some Mark IV models had ordinary horseshoe type magnetos driven by chain. The later Mark IV models, and all Mark V engines are fitted with Villiers fly-wheel magnetos.

These earlier models had no built-in clutch. A highly successful multi-plate friction clutch was produced for fitting on to the engine shaft to provide a free engine and thus allow smooth starting. It is unlikely that they are still in operation.

98 c.c. "Junior" de-luxe Engine. This popular model superseded the "Junior" engine and has proved highly successful when fitted to many types of auto-cycles. It differs from the more familiar deflector piston type in having a flat-top piston and detachable cylinder head. The ports are of a new design.

It has a bore and stroke of 50 mm. × 50 mm., roller big-end bearing, floating gudgeon pin and is fitted with a trouble-free fly-wheel magneto.

This highly efficient engine is most economical on petrol and oil and has the added advantage of being easily overhauled and decarbonized.

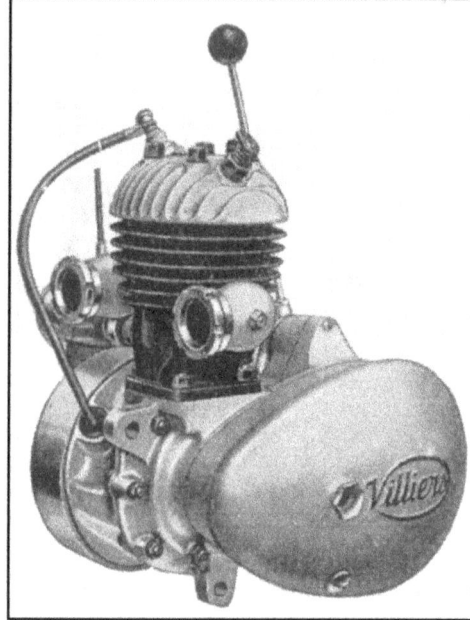

Fig. 6. The 98 c.c. and 125 c.c. Engine Unit

98 c.c. Mark 2 F (Autocycle) Engine. Specially designed for auto-cycles, this engine will master all main road hills without pedal assistance and on one gallon will traverse no fewer than 120 miles.

The bore and stroke are 47 and 57 mm. respectively; the weight, with fly-wheel magneto and carburettor, is only 31 lb. The deeply-finned cylinder has a detachable aluminium head, the latest type flat-top piston, ball bearings to crankshaft and clutch shaft, and roller-bearing big-end.

The fly-wheel magneto is of the latest pattern, providing lighting as well as ignition—the head lamp with a 6-volt, 12-watt main bulb and a 4-volt, 0·3-amp. parking bulb and tail lamp bulb. The flexible power is transmitted by roller chain in an oil bath to the two-plate clutch.

98 c.c. Mark 1 F Engine 2-speed Gear Unit (Ultra-lightweight Motor-cycle Engine). This is a 98 c.c. unit built in with a two-speed constant mesh gear-box. The bore is 47 mm. and the stroke 57 mm., and the specification is approximately as for the Mark 2 F. Starting is by kickstarter with a folding pedal, and the gears are operated by a sliding dog from the handlebar control lever. This unit for the ultra-lightweight motor-cycle weighs

TYPES OF VILLIERS TWO-STROKE ENGINES

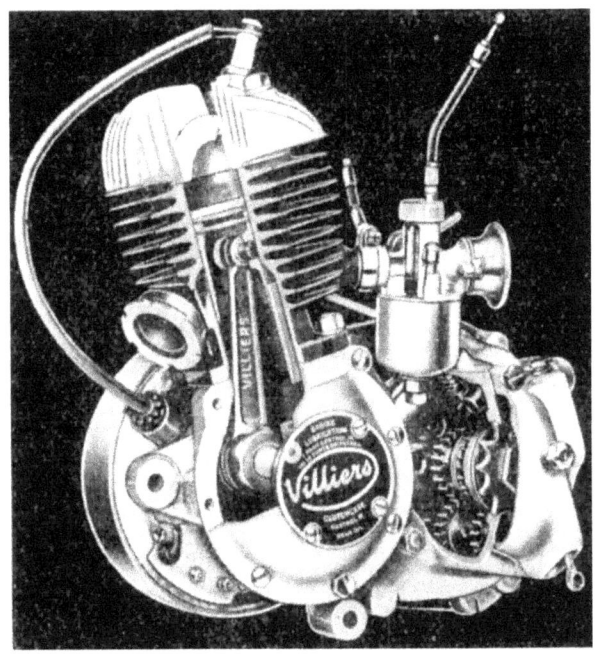

FIG. 7. THE 98 C.C. MARK 2 F ENGINE
Cut away to show internal details

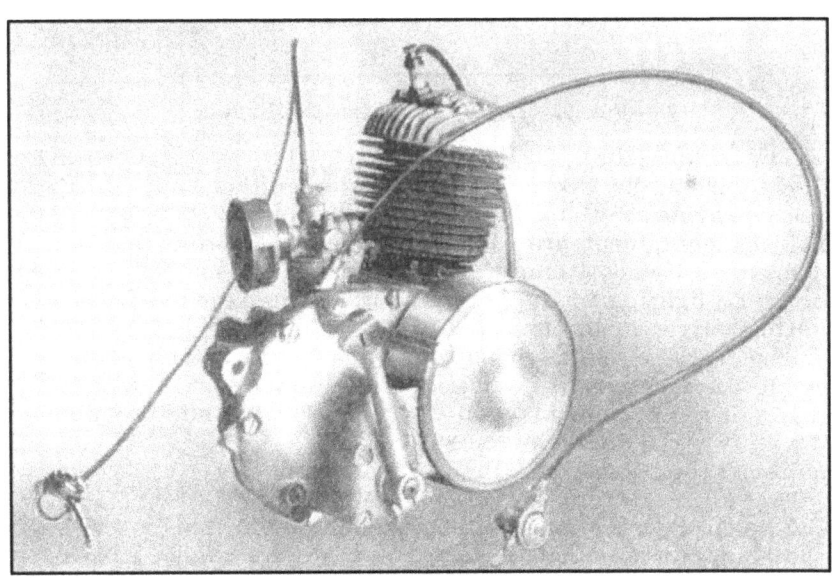

FIG. 8. THE 98 C.C. MARK 1 F ENGINE
AND GEAR-BOX UNIT

only 38 lb., and gives a petrol consumption of 140 miles to the gallon, or approximately twenty more miles to the gallon than the Mark 2 F.

98 c.c. Mark 4 F Engine 2-speed Gear Unit. This current production is similar in construction to the proved and popular Mark 1 F unit and has 47 mm. bore and 57 mm. stroke giving 2·8 h.p. at 4,000 r.p.m. The two-speed gears are controlled by a handlebar control and have ratios of 1·54 to 1, and 1 to 1.

FIG. 9. THE 98 C.C. MARK 6 F ENGINE

The carburettor is the "Junior" type 6/0 with jet size No. J.120, and taper needle No. 2½ type 6/0. The ignition and lighting are both provided by the 6-pole magneto for which two types of lighting equipment are available, namely; rectifier lighting for charging a 6-volt, 10 amp.-hour battery (the usual set supplied), or direct lighting to the lamps, the parking-light fed from a dry battery (Ever Ready type 800).

The rectifier set has head lamp, main bulb, 6 volt 12/12 watt small bayonet cap (s.b.c.) and pilot bulb 6 volt 3 watt m.b.c. The tail lamp main filament is 6 volt 3 watt and stop filament 6 volt 18 watt, double filament s.b.c.

This is the outstanding British lightweight motor-cycle engine.

98 c.c. Mark 6 F Engine 2-speed Gear Unit. This is similar to the Mark 4 F except that here the gears are changed by a foot lever fitted to the gearbox, but in the Mark 4 F the gears are controlled by a cable from the handlebar.

TYPES OF VILLIERS TWO-STROKE ENGINES

The 122 c.c. Mark 9 D Engine 3-speed Gear Unit. This combines a 122 c.c. engine with three-speed gear, clutch, and kick-starter, and has a bore of 50 mm. and a stroke of 62 mm. The latest flat top piston of similar design to the now famous 249 c.c. Mark XVIII A engine is employed. The cylinder is of cast iron and may be turned through 180 degrees so that the inlet port may be placed on either side and is thus convenient for fitting compactly in any frame. The same advantages apply to the head and the release valve.

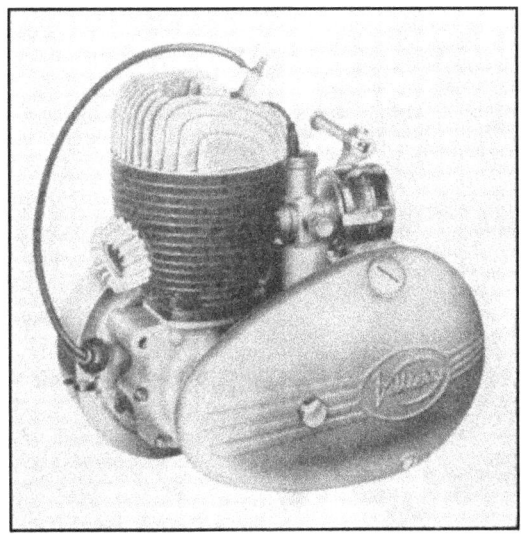

Fig. 10. The 147 c.c. Mark 30 C Engine

The engine has two exhaust ports, four transfer ports, a fully floating gudgeon pin, and a bronze bush fitted to the small end.

To reduce wear, the crankshaft is carried on three separate ball bearings, bronze bushes being used to retain compression. The big end consists of a full-row roller race around a hardened crankpin. The special Villiers fly-wheel magneto is entirely enclosed and has coils for direct lighting.

The gear-box is cast in one piece with the crankcase, and the gear lever is mounted direct on this casting. A single-plate cork clutch is employed and the primary drive is through a $\frac{3}{8}$-in. pitch chain requiring no adjustment and running in an aluminium oil bath case.

The lubrication employed is petroil and the unit complete weighs under 40 lb. and develops 4 h.p.

The machine fitted with this unit reaches well over 40 m.p.h. and has a fuel consumption of over 110 m.p.g. The mixture is supplied by a Villiers carburettor having either a single or double lever control.

122 c.c. Mark 10 D Engine 2-speed Gear Unit. The cylinder has a bore of 50 mm. and a stroke of 62 mm., a single exhaust, two transfer ports, a detachable aluminium cylinder head, and an aluminium flat-top piston with two rings.

The crankshaft has three ball bearings and the crankpin two rows of all-steel rollers.

The gear-box is three-speed with constant mesh gears; change is effected by an adjustable foot pedal and there is a folding kick-starter pedal. The magneto, of unique design, provides current for both ignition and lighting, the latter being of two types: (*a*) for direct lighting to bulbs and (*b*) for battery charging through a rectifier. The lighting is 30 and 24 watt respectively. The weight is only 50 lb.

FIG. 11. 196 C.C. MARK 2 E

122 c.c. Mark 12 D Engine 3-speed Gear Unit. This follows the design of the outstanding 9 D and 10 D engine units which it supersedes. The bore is 50 mm., the stroke 62 mm., and the power output at 4,000 r.p.m. is 4 b.h.p. The gear-box ratios are 1 to 1, 1·34 to 1, and 2·55 to 1, which give closer ratios than previous models. Gear changing by the right foot is positive and foolproof. The kickstarter mechanism is completely enclosed.

The carburettor is type S.19 with needle No. 3½ and throttle No. 2. The sparking plug variety is the same as that recommended for Mark 10 D. The magneto used is the latest 6-pole pattern providing for both lighting and ignition and whether for rectifier or direct lighting sets. Lubrication is particularly simple;

TYPES OF VILLIERS TWO-STROKE ENGINES 15

for the engine, the usual 1 to 16 oil/petrol ratio; for the gear-box and chain case, the recommended oil filled to the level plugs.

147 c.c. Engine. The first engine of this size, which commenced a new series of Villiers models, was known as the Mark VI C. From time to time, improvements and alterations have been made, and each successive change has been denoted by alteration to the mark on the engine, viz., the Mark VII C and the Mark VIII C models.

FIG. 12. 196 C.C. MARK 3 E ENGINE UNIT

These engines each have a bore of 55 mm. and a stroke of 62 mm.

The lubrication employed is petroil, which is a mixture of half a pint of oil with each gallon of petrol (see Chapter III on Lubrication).

This engine has a single exhaust pipe, a roller bearing big-end, and long phosphor-bronze bushes for the mainshafts.

The average petrol consumption obtainable in normal circumstances is 130 m.p.g., and the oil consumption is 2,000 m.p.g.

The Villiers fly-wheel magneto is fitted.

This engine is designed entirely from a utility point of view, and is fitted to many motor-cycles intended for this purpose.

147 c.c. Mark 30 C Engine 3-speed Gear Unit. This is similar, basically, to the famous Mark 12 D (see page 14) the difference being that the bore is 55 mm. and the stroke 62 mm. The water-proofed carburettor has a more efficient air cleaner and strangler, lubrication is by petroil with a ratio of 1 to 20, and direct lighting with 30/30 watt headlamp bulb, and rectifier lighting with 24/24 watt headlamp bulb are specified. There is a competition model Mark 29 C with a similar specification and a 4-speed competition model Mark 29 C/4 with ratios 1, 1·35, 2·3, and 3·47 to 1.

The 148 c.c. Long Stroke Engine (Mark XII C). This, a general utility economical long-stroke model (Fig. 10), has the following valuable features: double exhaust ports, full roller-bearing big-end, long phosphor-bronze main bearings, fully floating gudgeon pin, detachable inlet manifold, the Villiers fly-wheel magneto, the single lever carburettor, and petroil lubrication. It is also fitted with the Villiers patented inertia ring which is described on page 28.

Its bore is 53 mm. and stroke 67 mm. and approximate road performance as follows: speed 50 m.p.h., petrol consumption 90–100 m.p.g., and oil consumption 1,600 m.p.g.

This model could be obtained with a single exhaust port, Mark XV C, everything else being identical with the model described on page 15, and is illustrated in Fig. 10.

Two types of 172 c.c. sports engine with 57·15 mm. bore and 67 mm. stroke were introduced, viz., the "sports," with one-piece cylinders and old type deflector cast-iron pistons, and a "super-sports," with detachable cylinder head, aluminium piston, variable ignition-magneto, and a high compression aluminium-finned "Brooklands" cylinder. These models are not now made.

196 c.c. Mark 1 E Engine. The specification for this model, with the exception of the bore, is exactly the same as that of the 172 c.c. sports. The bore is 61 mm., and stroke 67 mm.

Principally this engine was intended for use in Germany, where a motor-cycle under 200 c.c. can be used without tax, but many British manufacturers fitted it because of its extreme reliability, and the fact that it could be handled successfully by inexpert riders.

This engine in a suitable machine gave a petrol consumption of approximately 90 m.p.g., and an oil consumption of 1,350 m.p.g.

Two alternative systems of lubrication are available—one by

TYPES OF VILLIERS TWO-STROKE ENGINES

the petroil method, and the other by the Villiers automatic system. (These systems are dealt with thoroughly later.)

196 c.c. Mark 2 E Engine. This engine, which is shown in Fig. 11, has a bore and stroke of 61 mm. × 67 mm., the total capacity being 196 c.c. A cast-iron piston and cylinder is employed, the latter being of the single exhaust port type. The engine has a roller-bearing big-end, long phosphor-bronze bushes for the mainshafts and a piston fitted with the Villiers patented inertia ring. The petroil system of lubrication is employed on this engine, and this is dealt with fully in Chapter III.

196 c.c. Mark 3 E Engine 3-speed Gear Unit. This combined engine and gear unit was introduced just prior to the war. It has a 59 mm. × 72 mm. bore and stroke, four transfer ports, a flat-topped piston, built-in three-speed constant-mesh gear-box, and a single-plate cork clutch. A 6-pole magneto with lighting coils is also fitted.

As will be seen from Fig. 12, the cylinder finning is carried very low down on the barrel and the exhaust ports are cast integrally with the barrel.

FIG. 13. 196 C.C. SUPER SPORTS

The three-speed gear-box is in unit with the engine, and is of sturdy design. The hand change lever is mounted directly on the right-hand side of the box. The drive to the clutch is by chain, which is enclosed in an aluminium oil-bath case. Ignition is by fly-wheel magneto, incorporating the latest Villiers 6-pole lighting system.

196 c.c. Super Sports Engine. This engine (Fig. 13) has the same bore and stroke as model 2 E described previously, but is a faster engine capable of a maximum speed of approximately 52 m.p.h., and of maintaining a higher average speed for longer distances. To attain this performance the cooling has to be very efficient,

Fig. 14. The 197 c.c. Mark 6 E Engine and Gear Unit

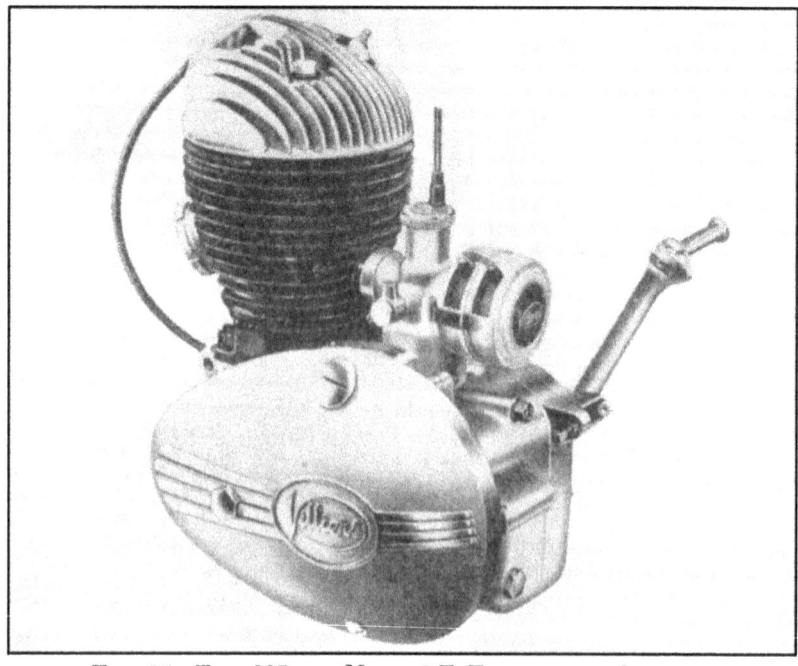

Fig. 15. The 197 c.c. Mark 8 E Engine and 3-speed Gear Unit—an Established Favourite

TYPES OF VILLIERS TWO-STROKE ENGINES

therefore a special aluminium piston and detachable alloy cylinder-head are employed. A departure is the fitting of an inertia ring, and the advantages of this fitment are explained in detail on page 31.

197 c.c. Mark 6 E Engine and Gear Unit. The design and construction follow those of the 122 c.c. Mark 10 D unit (page 14).

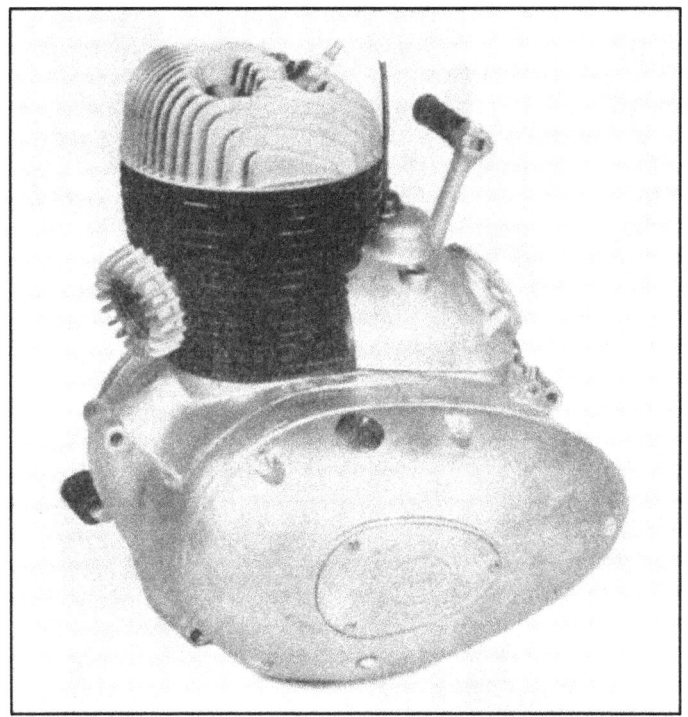

FIG. 16. THE 225 C.C. MARK 1 H ENGINE AND 4-SPEED GEAR UNIT

Bore is 59 mm. and stroke 72 mm. giving 8·4 h.p. at 4,000 r.p.m. The carburettor is type 4/5, jet size No. 1, and No. 4½ taper needle.

This model has now been superseded by Mark 8 E which is described below.

197 c.c. Mark 8 E Engine 3-speed Gear Unit. This is another outstanding achievement incorporating the latest developments. It has a bore of 59 mm. and stroke of 72 mm. and gear-box ratios of 1 to 1, 1·34 to 1 and 2·55 to 1. The power output at 4,000 r.p.m. is 7·5 B.H.P.

Fig. 18. The 249 c.c. (2¼ h.p.) Air Cooled Engine

Fig. 17. The 247 c.c. Engine

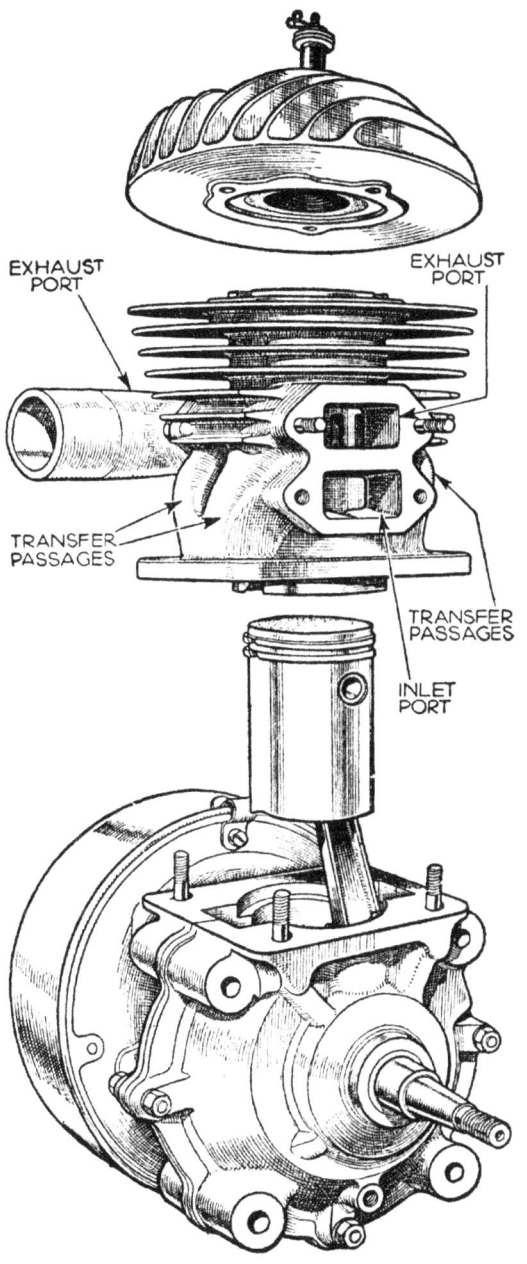

Fig. 19. An "Exploded" View of the Mark XVIII A Villiers Engine, Showing the "Deflectorless" Piston and the Disposition of the Cylinder Ports (2 Exhaust and 4 Transfer)

(From "The Motor Cycle," London)

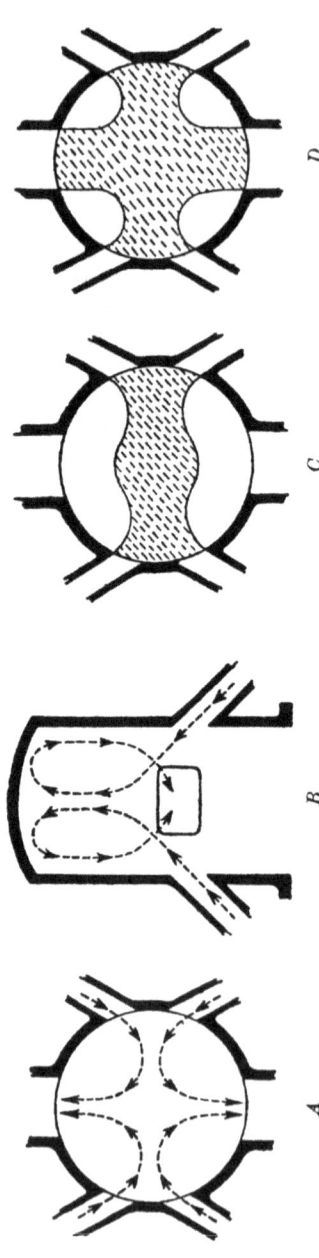

FIG. 20. DIAGRAMS ILLUSTRATING THE THEORETICAL GAS FLOW IN THE FLAT-TOPPED-PISTON TYPE VILLIERS ENGINE

A shows how the gases from each pair of ports impinge on each other and spread out across the cylinder in a horizontal plane. *B* shows how the combined gas streams impinge on each other and go up the cylinder in a vertical plane. *C* shows the zones on a section just above the exhaust port, the shaded part being the upward or inlet zone, and the unshaded the downward or exhaust zone. *D* shows the zones on a section near the top of the cylinder, where the upward zone takes the form of a cross, due to the fact that the gases from the two pairs of transfer ports impinge together as well as individually.

(*From "The Motor Cycle," London*)

TYPES OF VILLIERS TWO-STROKE ENGINES

The carburettor is type S.25 using a needle No. 3½ and throttle No. 3. The sparking plug is the same type as that used in the Mark 6 E.

Lighting and ignition are by 6-pole magneto providing both direct and rectifier lighting, as described for the Mark 12 D engine gear unit.

197 c.c. Mark 8 E/4 Engine 4-speed Gear Unit. This is similar to the standard 8 E engine but with 4 gear-box ratios of 1 to 1, 1·35 to 1, 1·8 to 1, and 2·93 to 1.

There is a competition model of the 8 E, namely the Mark 7 E with a similar specification and the Mark 7 E/4 with 4-speed ratios of 1·35, 2·3, and 3·47 to 1. For light 3-wheeled cars there is the Mark 8 E/R with a 3-speed and reverse unit and fan cooling.

225 c.c. Mark 1 H Engine 4-speed Gear Unit. This streamlined model has a bore of 63 mm. and a stroke of 72 mm., a flat-top 3-ring piston, a 4-journal ball-bearing crankshaft, a multi-plate cork clutch, a Type S.25 totally enclosed carburettor with shrouded air filter and a 4-speed constant mesh gear-box, with ratios of 1, 1·32, 1·9 and 3·06 to 1. It has rectifier and battery lighting with 24/24-watt headlamps.

247 c.c. (2¼ h.p.) Engine. The original model of this series was known as the Mark VI A, which had a cast-iron cylinder (fixed head) and piston, single exhaust port and petroil lubrication. The bore was 67 mm. and the stroke 70 mm.

Various improvements produced the Mark VII A model which was followed by the Mark VIII A, both of which had cast-iron cylinders and pistons. With the Mark VIII A model came the introduction of the window-type transfer port, twin exhaust ports, and the detachable inlet-manifold.

Automatic lubrication, detachable heads, and aluminium pistons proved outstanding features of the Mark IX A and X A and with the auxiliary fly-wheel on the driving side gave a delightful smoothness especially at low speed. This engine has a petrol consumption of 90 m.p.g. and an oil consumption of 2,000 m.p.g.

Almost similar to the X A is the XVI A, the difference being a three-bolt head, as against a four-bolt, and petroil lubrication.

The 249 c.c. (2½ h.p.) Air-cooled Engine. This model (Fig. 18) is known as the Mark XIV A long stroke engine, has a speed of 60 m.p.h., a petrol consumption of 70–80 m.p.g., and of oil, 1,800 to 2,000 m.p.g. Having an aluminium alloy cylinder head and a piston of an entirely new light alloy, the cooling is most efficient. The patented inertia ring is fitted, which prevents the gumming up of the two rings below it. The auxiliary fly-wheel ensures the

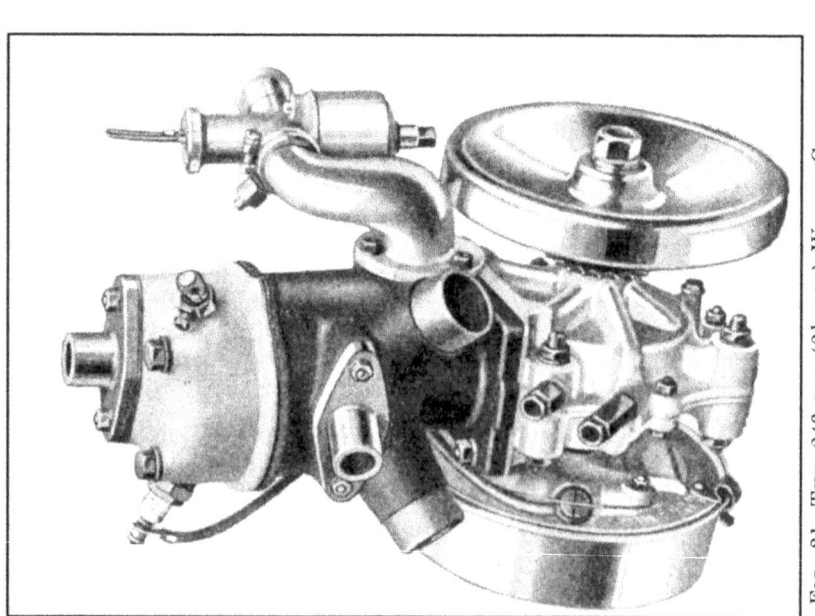

Fig. 21. The 249 c.c. (2¼ h.p.) Water Cooled Engine Mark XIV a-ry

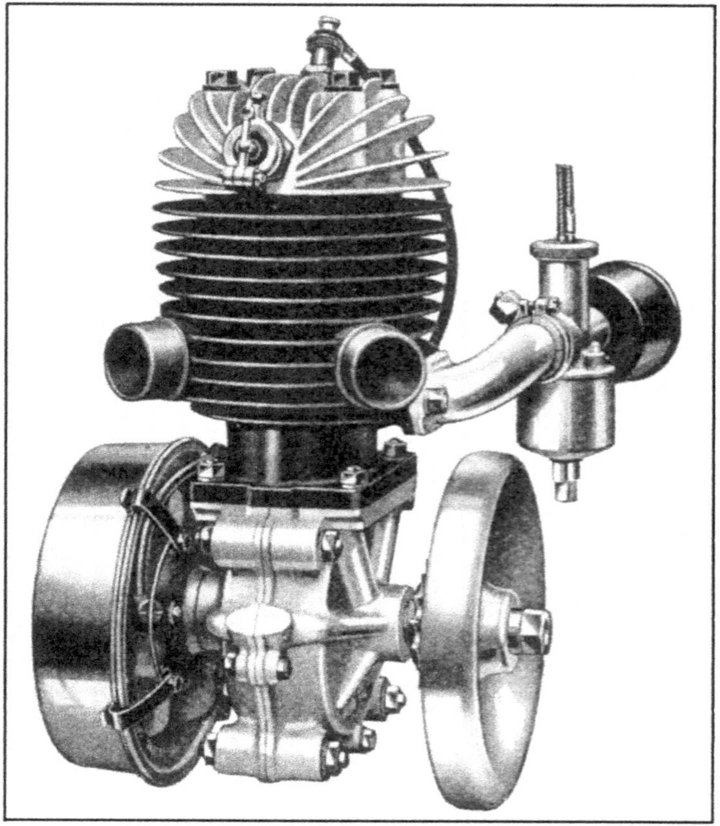

Fig. 22. 346 c.c. Long-stroke Mark XIV B

TYPES OF VILLIERS TWO-STROKE ENGINES

smoothest running and the two-lever Villiers carburettor the best speed with economy, due to the automatic compensating action.
Lubrication is by petroil or by the automatic lubricator which increases the flow of oil as the load becomes greater. The bore is 63 mm. and the stroke 80 mm.

The 249 c.c. (2½ h.p.) Water-cooled Engine Mark XIV A-RY.

This model (Fig. 21) is a revelation in power, flexibility, and silence. The cooling by water ensures good pulling power at very low speeds and under severe tests, with a suitable radiator, it has been found impossible to make the water boil.

The power developed is 11½ h.p., maximum speed 60 m.p.h., petrol consumption 60 to 90 m.p.g., and oil consumption 2,000 m.p.g. It has a detachable cylinder head of improved design (see Fig. 21), a special aluminium alloy piston with deflector shaped head to give the greatest efficiency and this is fitted with the patent inertia ring. An auxiliary fly-wheel ensures smooth slow running and the automatic lubricating system is standard.

249 c.c. Mark XVII A and XVIII A Engines and all Current Models.

The Villiers Company has produced a revolutionary design with completely original design of ports and flat-topped piston.

The 249 c.c. Mark XVII A was the first model introduced and was quickly followed by Mark XVIII A which had an improved crankshaft assembly. Both models had petroil lubrication.

The advantages gained by this unique design are as follows: (1) the symmetrical piston is lighter, machined to closer limits, (2) decreased weight of the piston exerts less load upon the bearings, (3) rattle is eliminated because there is no piston tilt, (4) decrease in the surface area of the combustion chamber leads to increased thermal efficiency, (5) more even distribution of metal, and so distortion is far less likely, (6) the flat piston top (as opposed to the common type with a deflector top) provides better balance of the piston above the gudgeon pin, (7) the arrangement of ports on opposite sides provides a far better distribution of heat and again reduces the risk of distortion, (8) carbonization of oil on certain areas of the cylinder wall is avoided, (9) no gumming up of piston rings, and (10) the sparking plug can be placed in an accessible position without efficiency being affected.

In short, the engine runs much quieter, will stand up to hard work with less fear of distortion, less oil is used because of the better conduction of heat, and one-third more power is obtained from the same petrol consumption.

There are four transfer ports, two each side of the cylinder, and meeting the cylinder in an upward direction. There are also two exhaust ports situated exactly opposite one another, see Fig. 19.

The efficiency depends upon the directional aim of the gases coming through the transfer ports and going out at the exhaust. The mixtures of gases coming through the four oppositely placed ports impinge upon one another, and so force themselves up to the top of the cylinder, in the same way as a double jet acetylene burner produces the fan-like flame. The exhaust gas, which in reality is being displaced, is forced downward between the currents of new combustible gases and out at the exhaust ports. As the joined column of fresh gas reaches the cylinder head it is turned downward in two streams, and still further forces out the last volumes of exhaust gases. After this has happened the piston has risen far enough to close all ports, and the new gases are compressed.

Reference to Fig. 20 will make clearer the theoretical flow of gas.

342 c.c. Mark VI B to X B Engines. The VI B and VII B were an early issue with bore and stroke of 79 mm. × 70 mm. and had fixed cylinder heads, single exhausts, plain bearings, and cast-iron pistons, lubrication being by the drip-feed method. Then followed Mark VIII B, IX B, and X B with the improvements of detachable aluminium heads, aluminium pistons with floating gudgeons, twin exhausts, inertia rings, and automatic lubrication.

346 c.c. Mark XIV B Engine. This engine followed the Mark X B and has a bore and stroke of 70 mm. × 90 mm. respectively, and is shown in Fig. 22. An aluminium alloy cylinder head is used, and the alloy piston is entirely new. The bearings are as described for the 2 E engine. Alternative systems of lubrication are available on this engine, i.e. the petroil system or the automatic system. This engine is fitted with the Villiers patented inertia ring.

353 c.c. Mark 28 B Engine and 3-speed Gear Unit. This engine of 75 mm. × 80 mm. gives a b.h.p. of 8·25 at 3,500 r.p.m. and is popular for use in light three-wheeled cars because it has air cooling with a fan and provides a reverse. The ratios for this purpose are 4·86, 8·95 and 18·95 to 1. The weight of the engine is 83 lb. and it is in current production with all the latest developments which have brought the Villiers engine to the top.

Outstanding Performances. Whilst dealing with the petrol consumption and capabilities of the various Villiers engines, it is interesting to recall the following feats recently accomplished, which, at the time, created an enormous stir amongst motor-cyclists.

TYPES OF VILLIERS TWO-STROKE ENGINES

One of these was a ride from London to Edinburgh by a lady on a motor-cycle fitted with the Villiers 147 c.c. engine. The test was officially conducted by the Auto Cycle Union, and the machine used was a perfectly standard model taken from an agent's stock without the knowledge of the manufacturers. The distance between London and Edinburgh is 393 miles, and the petrol consumption averaged 214 m.p.g. The total cost of fuel and oil used on this journey was only 3s. 4d., which illustrates very forcibly the economy of the utility two-stroke motor-cycle.

Another well-known performance was the climbing of Snowdon up the railway track by three motor-cycles fitted with the Villiers 172 c.c. super-sports engines. The average gradient was 1 in 7·4 over a distance of 5 miles, and the time taken by these machines was only 22 minutes.

Villiers engines apparently thrive on mountains. Following the performance on Snowdon, another machine, with the same type of engine, was ridden to the summit of Ben Nevis, (4,400 ft.). The time taken was 2 hours 2 minutes, which is remark-

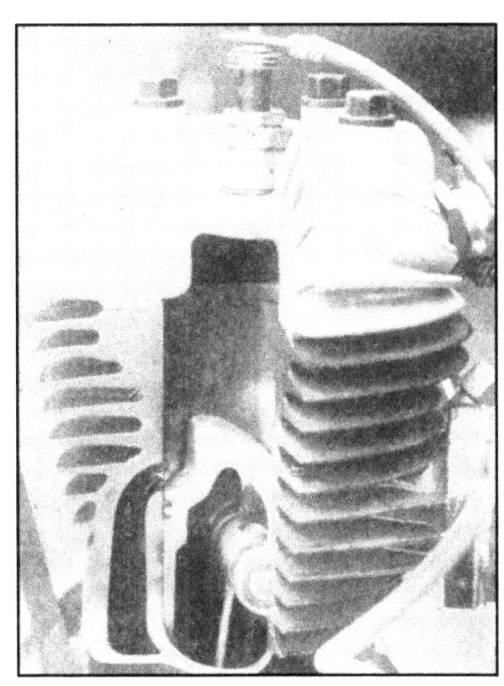

FIG. 23. CYLINDER WITH DETACHABLE HEAD
Note the deflector on the piston used on the older models and on a few of the current ones

able when it is remembered that the greater portion of the journey was accomplished in deep snow.

One reason for the remarkable hill climbing powers of a two-stroke engine, is the fact that a power impulse is delivered at every revolution, and the power output therefore remains high even when the speed falls greatly. This gives the Villiers engine a remarkable pulling capacity.

It should be understood that the figures given for petrol and oil consumption are conservative estimates and are only approximate.

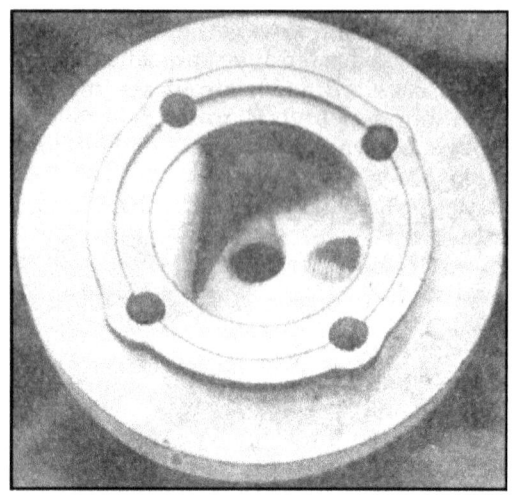

Fig. 24. Underside View of Detachable Head on Villiers Cylinder

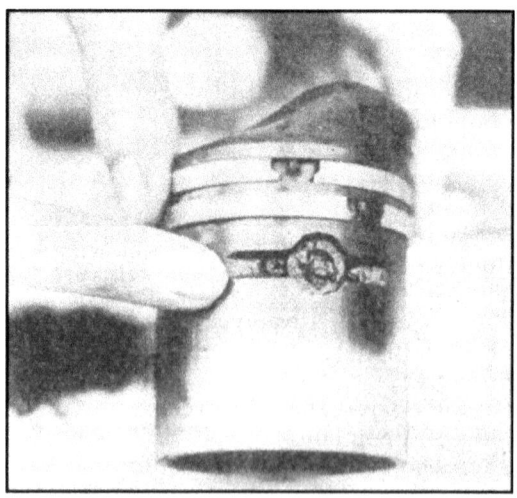

Fig. 25. Method of Holding Fixed Type of Gudgeon Pin

Note also the small pegs retaining the rings in their correct positions

TYPES OF VILLIERS TWO-STROKE ENGINES

THE PRINCIPAL COMPONENTS DESCRIBED

The Cylinder. This part is made of cast iron, and in the models in which a detachable head is employed this head is made from a special aluminium alloy.

On the cylinder and head are thin fins for the purpose of radiating the heat generated by combustion and so keeping the engine cool. The purpose of using an aluminium alloy head

Fig. 26. THE VILLIERS CRANKSHAFT ASSEMBLY

is to assist this cooling, because on some models, where heat is great, it is necessary to dissipate this heat quicker.

Careful calculation is undertaken to arrive at the correct area and spacing of these fins.

Various ports, previously described, are cast in the cylinder, and the inside of the head is shaped to give the most efficient volume and size of combustion chamber. Figs. 23 and 53 show very clearly the design and construction of a cylinder with detachable head. The internal diameter of the cylinder is known as the bore of the engine.

The Piston. These are of cast iron or special aluminium alloy, according to the type of engine to which they are fitted. The alloy pistons are usually fitted in high speed engines, because they lessen the reciprocating weight, and allow higher revolutions.

In the older models, the engine had 3 ports; for inlet, for exhaust, and for transfer of the gases from crankcase to combustion chamber. The piston head was shaped as a deflector (Fig. 23) but in 1934 a unique design was adopted in which there were 2 exhaust and 4 transfer ports enabling a flat-topped piston (Fig. 20) to be used with much greater efficiency.

At the top of the piston are two or more piston rings which are free in their grooves, but which through spring tension

TECHNICAL DATA

Model		Bore × Stroke	Approximate Road Performance		
			Max. Speed m.p.h.	Petrol Consumption m.p.g.	Oil Consumption m.p.g.
98 c.c.	"Midget" Engine . .	50 mm. × 50 mm.	30	120	2,000
122 c.c.	Mark 9 D	50 mm. × 62 mm.	40	115	2,000
147 c.c.	Mark VIII C	55 mm. × 62 mm.	40	130	2,000
148 c.c.	Mark XII C .	53 mm. × 67 mm.	50	90–100	1,600
196 c.c.	Mark 1 E	61 mm. × 67 mm.	45	90	1,600
196 c.c.	Mark 2 E	61 mm. × 67 mm.	45	90	1,600
196 c.c.	Super-Sports	61 mm. × 67 mm.	50–52	90	1,600
196 c.c.	Mark 3 E	59 mm. × 72 mm.	55	80–85	1,600
249 c.c.	Mark XIV A	63 mm. × 80 mm.	60	70–80	1,800–2,000
249 c.c.	Water-cooled	63 mm. × 80 mm.	60	70–90	2,000
249 c.c.	Mark XVIII A	63 mm. × 80 mm.	62	70–90	2,000
346 c.c.	Mark XIV B	70 mm. × 90 mm.	60	70–80	1,800–2,000
POST-WAR MODELS					
98 c.c.	Mark 1 F	47 mm. × 57 mm.	40	140	2,000
98 c.c.	Mark 2 F	47 mm. × 57 mm.	30	120	2,000
98 c.c.	Mark 4 F	47 mm. × 57 mm.	38–40	120	2,000
122 c.c.	Mark 10 D	50 mm. × 62 mm.	45	110	2,000
122 c.c.	Mark 12 D	50 mm. × 62 mm.	45–48	110	2,000
147 c.c.	Mark 30 C	55 mm. × 62 mm.	45	100	1,800
148 c.c.	Mark 31 C	57 mm. × 58 mm.	45	100	1,800
173 c.c.	Mark 2 L	59 mm. × 63·5 mm.	50	110	1,600
197 c.c.	Mark 6 E	59 mm. × 72 mm.	55	90	1,600
197 c.c.	Mark 8 E	59 mm. × 72 mm.	55–60	95	1,600
197 c.c.	Mark 9 E	59 mm. × 72 mm.	60	85	1,600
225 c.c.	Mark 1 H	63 mm. × 72 mm.	60	80	1,600
249 c.c.	Mark 2 T	50 mm. × 63·5 mm.	70	85	1,500
324 c.c.	Mark 3 T	57 mm. × 63·5 mm.	75	80	1,500

bear against the cylinder walls, and so make a seal which prevents the combustion pressure in the cylinder head blowing past the piston. It is necessary to prevent the rings rotating in their grooves, because by so doing they might catch in one of the cylinder ports, and this is done by means of a small peg fitting into

TYPES OF VILLIERS TWO-STROKE ENGINES

the slot in the piston ring. These pegs, very important, may be observed in Figs. 25 and 36. Later models have a key (see page 50).

Inertia Ring. The fitting of the Villiers Patented Inertia Ring (Fig. 33) to the latest models is one of the most important improvements in two-stroke engine designs for many years.

The object of the inertia ring is to prevent the gumming up of the ordinary piston rings, and it achieves this object in a very simple manner. In practice it was found that a film of oil formed above the piston rings and gradually became burnt and carboned, eventually fixing the rings solid in their grooves.

The inertia ring which is fitted above the top piston-ring is designed so that it cannot touch the cylinder walls and is permitted to have a slight up and down movement and to rotate freely. This movement prevents any portion of oil forming above the piston ring and so keeps the ring quite free.

Gudgeon Pin. Working in its bearings in the piston is the gudgeon pin, which acts as a pivot for the small end of the connecting rod.

In the early type Villiers engines the gudgeon pin was fixed in the piston, but in the later models it is fully floating, which means that it can rotate in the piston bosses as well as in the connecting rod. Soft metal pads are fitted in both ends of the floating gudgeon pin to prevent it damaging the cylinder walls. The gudgeon pins in flat-topped pistons are located by circlips.

The Connecting Rod. This acts as a link between the piston and the crankshaft to convert up and down movement of the piston into rotating movement of the crankshaft.

The connecting rod is made from a very strong steel forging, and is of such a design that it cannot bend or collapse under the heavy combustion pressure. Its bearing at the small-end for the gudgeon pin is a plain phosphor-bronze bush. At the big-end it runs on a roller-bearing.

The Crankshaft. This component is built up from two shafts joined together by means of a crank pin, which is the part on which the big-end of the connecting rod actually takes its bearing.

The distance between the centre line of the shaft and the centre line of the crank pin is known as the " throw."

The position of the crankshaft is fixed by the bearings in the crankcase, and the crank pin describes a circle round the shaft. The diameter of this imaginary circle is known as the " stroke " of the engine, and is equivalent to twice the throw.

CHAPTER III
LUBRICATION

CORRECT lubrication of an engine is of the utmost importance. The useful life and the amount of good service an engine will give depend almost entirely upon the way in which it is lubricated, especially during the first stages of its life.

The present-day two-stroke engine is so reliable, that the owner is required to do very little towards its upkeep, the only constant attention that is asked of him being to keep a plentiful supply of oil in the tank, and to see that a regular quantity is given to the engine at all times.

Patent Castrol XL, which is obtainable at all first-class garages, has been found by experiment to give good results on Villiers engines, and as it is advisable always to use one particular brand of oil, and not to change from one to another, Villiers riders are recommended to adopt this brand regularly.

On the earlier Villiers engines, lubrication was usually effected by means of a semi-automatic drip feed, or by the petroil method. The methods employed are: petroil in the 98 c.c., 122 c.c., 147 c.c., 148 c.c., 197 c.c., 225 c.c. and on some 172 c.c., 196 c.c., 249 c.c., and 346 c.c. engines, and the patented Villiers automatic lubrication system on the Super-Sports, Mark IX A 249 c.c. and 346 c.c., Mark IX B, and some 196 and 172 c.c. Sports. The patented automatic system will be described later.

The Semi-automatic Drip Feed. As stated above, this is not employed on present-day Villiers engines, but as it is in use on many old models, the following brief description will not be out of place. A lubricator is fitted into the oil compartment of the tank, and consists of a hand-pump connected to a drip-feed chamber, which has a glass top for the purpose of observing the oil supply. The lower end of the pump reaches to the bottom of the oil tank. This pump is worked by a spring (see diagram, Fig. 27). When the plunger is depressed, oil enters into the barrel of the pump and is forced out at the top into the sight-feed chamber by the upward action of this spring. An adjustable screw at the side (or top in some models) controls the flow of oil into the chamber. By way of the bottom of the chamber, the oil is lead through copper piping to the crankcase.

The oil supply varies according to the use to which the machine is put; 25 to 30 drops per minute is perhaps a good average setting.

LUBRICATION

The Petroil System. This is undoubtedly the simplest method and is used on all current models.

Oil should be mixed with the petrol before the fuel is placed into the tank so that there is no danger of the two fluids not mixing. For the older models half a pint of oil should be mixed

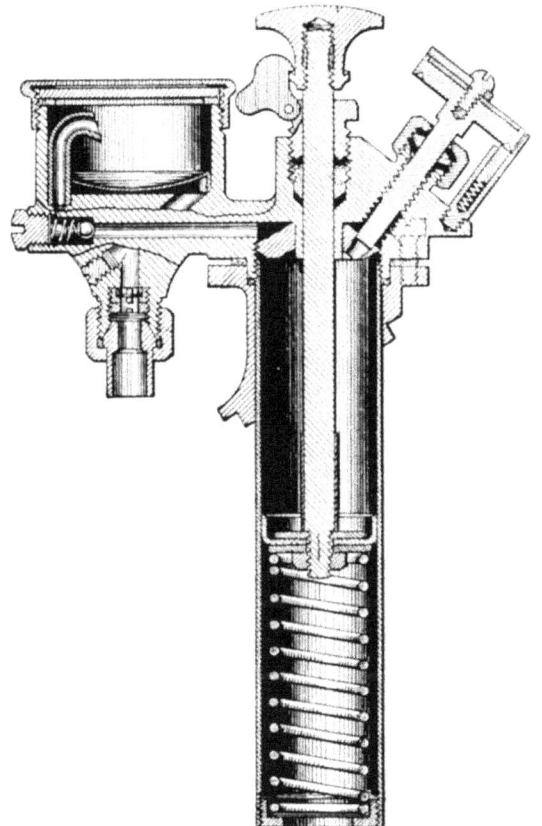

FIG. 27. THE DRIP FEED TYPE OF LUBRICATOR

with each gallon of petrol (i.e. proportion of 1 part oil to 16 petrol) but the modern engines use a mixture of 1 part oil to 20 parts petrol. The rider then has nothing whatever to do with the lubrication until he again fills up with petrol, in which case oil must always be mixed with it in the above proportion. The reason that this method of lubrication can be employed is that with a two-stroke engine the fuel is first of all taken into the crankcase, where it is compressed and then pumped to the cylinder.

By this route, oil mixed with the fuel is able to lubricate the bearings in the crankcase and the cylinder walls, and, in fact, every other part needing lubrication in the engine.

This method is particularly suitable for small two-stroke

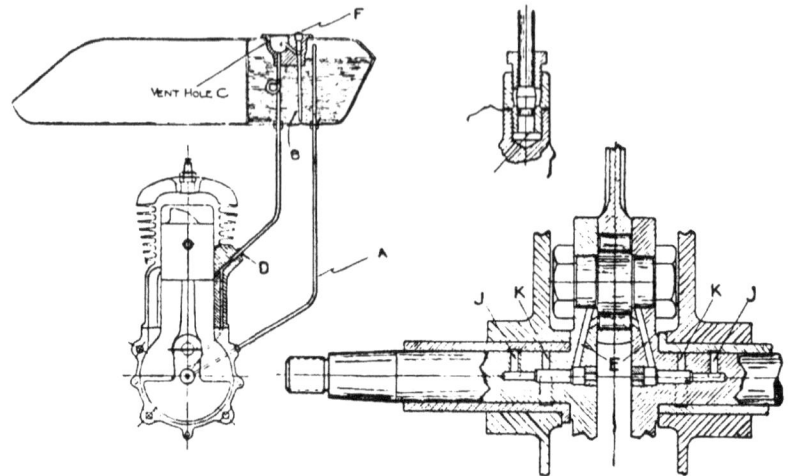

Fig. 28A. Diagram of Villiers Automatic Lubrication System (Mark I Pattern)

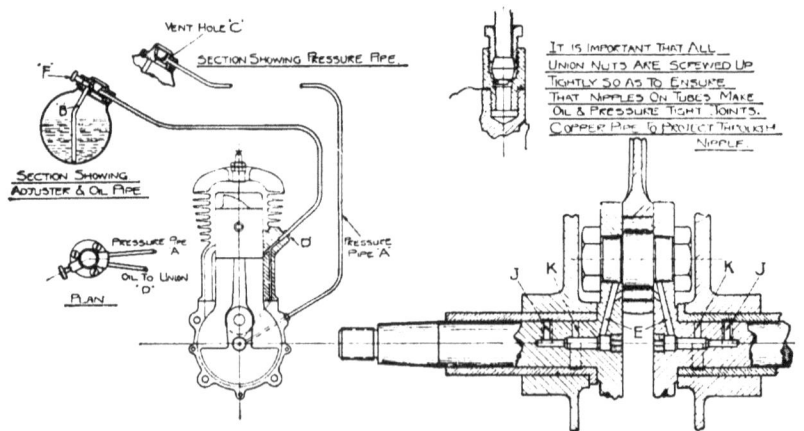

Fig. 28B. Diagram of Villiers Automatic Lubrication System (Mark II Pattern)

engines, but has been found not to be so efficient in the older high-speed models and for which a pressure system is better.

The Villiers Patented Automatic Lubrication System. This

LUBRICATION

system was designed to overcome certain inherent disadvantages of the mechanical oil pump, and the hand-operated system.

The mechanical pump delivers oil only in proportion to the engine speed, and the hand pump according to the amount of manual work done.

In the Villiers automatic system, variations in the crankcase pressure are utilized to supply oil direct to each bearing. As the pressure in the crankcase varies according to the throttle opening, it will be seen that the more the throttle is open and, consequently, the heavier the load on the engine, the greater is the oil supply, which is an ideal arrangement. Reference to Figs. 28A and 28B, together with the following description, will make the circulation system of the oil quite clear.

Oil under pressure from the crankcase passes along the centre of the shafts to the holes J, which register with grooves in the crankcase bushes as the piston descends. This oil is transferred through holes drilled in the crankcase to a union situated in front of the crankcase. From this point it is conveyed through the pressure pipe A to the top of the oil tank, raising the pressure in this, and forcing oil up the pipe B in the same way as soda water is forced up the centre tube of a soda syphon. The oil passes the regulating screw F, and issues into the cup of the sight feed. From this the oil descends to the engine through a union D on the front of the cylinder. Here the oil divides, part of it being sucked through a hole in the cylinder wall uncovered by the piston, and the rest passing down to the crankcase, where it is again divided between the two main bearings. Grooves in these register with ports K in the crankshafts when the piston is ascending, and the surplus oil is sucked through the drilled oilways E to the big-end. When the engine stops, the pressure in the tank is released via the main bearings of the engine, but oil would continue to syphon out of the tank into the engine if provision were not made for this. The vent hole C prevents this, as, by permitting air to pass into the sight-feed cup from the tank, it enables the oil in the pipe D to drain down to the engine without sucking further oil up pipe B. There is a continuous flow of air through vent C, while the engine is running, and this passes down to the engine with the oil, keeping the sight-feed cup clear. *It is of the utmost importance that the size of the vent hole should not be altered.*

The adjusting screw F is usually set, when the motor-cycle is sent out, to supply rather more oil than is normally required. After running 300 miles, this should be screwed in slightly to reduce the oil supply.

The correct setting has been obtained when a faint blue haze of smoke issues from the exhaust pipe under normal road conditions.

The sight feed is provided to ascertain if oil is flowing, and not to gauge the quantity. Three types of Villiers lubricators have been made; the one illustrated in Fig. 28A is the Mark I pattern, and was principally fitted by manufacturers who used a compartment in the main fuel tank for their oil supply. The Mark II pattern, illustrated in Fig. 28B, is employed when a separate oil

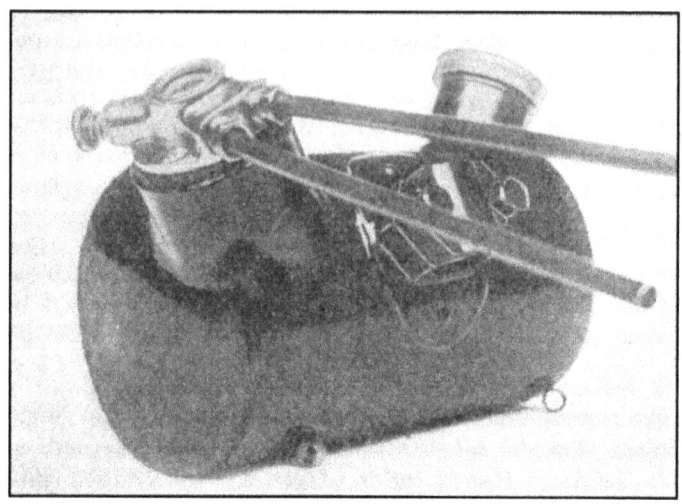

FIG. 29. SEPARATE OIL TANK WITH AUTOMATIC LUBRICATOR
This tank is used in conjunction with the Mark II oil pump illustrated in Fig. 28B

tank is used, such as that shown in Fig. 29. The Mark III is identical in operation with the Mark II pattern, the main difference being that the lubricator itself in the tank has no sight feed, as the Mark III pattern is usually fitted with the oil tank totally enclosed. The difference is merely a matter of arrangement, but the principle of both is precisely the same. The Mark II pattern can be converted for petroil use by the manufacturers.

Running Instructions for the Villiers Automatic Lubricator. All the unions of the oil pipes, both at the lubricator and engine ends, are of the solderless type; each nipple has a taper at either end, and there is a corresponding internal cone on the unions and nuts. When the nuts are screwed up they tend to squeeze in the nipples, making them grip on the pipes. It is important always to keep these unions tight.

From the description given it will be seen that the system **works** by pressure, and therefore it is important that this be

LUBRICATION

always maintained in the tank; consequently the unions must be tight and there should be no air leak from the oil compartment. Special attention should be paid to screwing the filler cap down firmly, and making quite sure that it seats on its leather washer. The filler cap, of course, must have no vent hole such as is drilled in the cap of a petrol tank. A common cause of pressure leakage is due to enamel on the threads of the filler-cap collar preventing the cap from screwing down fully. A similar trouble can arise from the washer being creased. It should always lie quite flat. The average pressure in the tank is about 4 lb. per sq. in. under normal conditions, and this pressure must be maintained. Failure to comply with this will result in over-oiling at low speeds, and a shortage of oil at speeds over 25–30 m.p.h.

If one of the unions is thought to be leaking, it is a good plan to smear it with oil and start up the engine.

Bubbles will form on the oil at the tank or crankcase unions if a leakage is present, or, at the cylinder union, the oil will be sucked in.

Should the lubricator continue to deliver oil after the engine has stopped, this is due to syphonic action caused by the small vent hole being choked. The vent hole, which is very small, should be cleaned with a single strand of Bowden wire. If the sight-feed bowl fills with oil, this is due to an air leak under the sight-feed glass.

Setting the Oil Supply. The flow of oil varies automatically according to the engine load and throttle opening, and is self-adjusting within reasonable variations of temperature. The best setting is obtained by adjusting the regulating screw to give a faint haze of smoke from the exhaust pipe when the machine is pulling normally in top gear along a level road. In very cold weather it is advisable to increase this setting.

CHAPTER IV

HOW TO HANDLE THE VILLIERS ENGINE

IF satisfactory running and long life are desired of Villiers engines, it is essential that they be handled intelligently, and that due regard be paid to lubrication and to minor adjustments when necessary. Villiers engines, it is true, are of such robust and simple construction that they will withstand a vast amount of abuse, but prolonged abuse and neglect inevitably result in serious wear and unsatisfactory service. It behoves the owner of a Villiers engine to treat it with the respect due to it. In this way a maximum amount of pleasure will be derived, and a minimum of expenditure incurred.

The Controls. The controls of the Villiers engine are few in number. They comprise the throttle operating lever, which regulates the speed and is situated on the right-hand side of the handlebars, (where there is a two-lever carburettor, this is supplemented by an independent control for the jet); and the compression release valve (the counterpart of the exhaust valve lifter in the four-stroke engine) fitted, as a rule, on the left-hand side.

To Start Up. First of all the petrol tap must be opened, and, on a machine with automatic lubrication, the oil regulator should be correctly adjusted.

When the engine is *cold* the carburettor must be flooded by depressing the " tickler " on the top of the float chamber. If a Villiers carburettor is fitted, the lever controlling the jet must be turned towards the " Rich " position. The throttle control lever should be opened a quarter, and the release valve lever lifted. It is not always necessary to lift the release valve, especially in the case of small engines, but it will be found advisable to do so on the larger models.

The engine should now be turned over slowly several times by depressing the kick starter, so drawing a charge of gas into the cylinder. Now give one strong kick on the starter pedal, and drop the release valve as the pedal nears the bottom. The engine should now fire, but if it fails to do so flood the carburettor again and repeat the above operation.

Never flood the carburettor when starting a warm engine.

In any case, when flooding, it is not necessary to let the petrol drip for a long time, but is sufficient if it just oozes over the top

HOW TO HANDLE THE VILLIERS ENGINE

of the chamber. Should the engine prove obstinate it is probably due to the sparking plug, and this should be taken out and examined (see page 74), but before examining the plug it is a good plan to try several vigorous kicks with the throttle three-quarter open. This will weaken an over-rich mixture, and frequently enables a start to be made. If the sparking plug points are oily, this will indicate that the engine was over-oiled on its last run, and that a surplus has accumulated in the crankcase. The plug points in this case must be thoroughly cleaned. If the points are just wet, this will indicate that a quantity of neat petrol has accumulated in the crankcase, probably due to flooding the carburettor too much. In either case the crankcase must be drained by means of the little screw on the chain sprocket side. The sparking plug may be tested when out of the cylinder by laying it on top of the cylinder head with the high tension cable connected to it, and turning the engine over slowly, which should produce a sparking at the plug points.

On a machine with no kick-starter, the engine can be set in motion quite easily by running the machine with bottom or middle gear engaged and the release valve lever lifted. When the machine is under motion the release valve lever can be dropped, and the engine will then fire. The clutch can be lifted immediately so that the engine will continue to run, and the machine itself can be brought to a standstill.

Just a word here on the question of Bowden controls. If the cables do not receive periodical attention an engine will assume a tendency to be very erratic, due to the fact that the throttle will not respond immediately to any movement of the control lever owing to slackness in the cables. They should be kept adjusted on the carburettor or control lever by means of the screwed cable stops provided for this purpose, and lubricated.

"**Running-in**" **a New Engine.** When an engine is assembled the bearings are made as close a fit as is reasonably possible. Owing to the crystalline nature of metal, an extensive and prolonged smooth rubbing will compress the bearing surfaces of the metal together until they attain a glass-like uniformity and hardness. During this process, of course, a certain amount of play arises in the bearings—just sufficient for good running fits. Thereafter wear is very slow. But imagine what will happen if the bearings are straightaway subjected to violent friction and heat. Instead of the surfaces becoming glassy, they will rapidly wear down and become scored or abraded, and continue to be rather soft. Another important point to consider is the fact that until there are good running fits throughout the engine, oil will be unable to find its way about properly over the bearing surfaces, which, in consequence, will remain partially dry if the engine is unduly worked, with the attendant danger of seizure. Distortion through overheating is also liable to arise. Distortion is of two kinds—temporary and permanent. If permanent distortion of the cylinder takes place, an engine will never be fully efficient afterwards. All Villiers engines are bench tested before leaving the manufacturers; but as this running is not great, the rider should restrain his desire to drive the engine hard until at least 500 miles on the road have been covered.

Cruising Speed. Every Villiers engine has what, for want of a better name, may be called its cruising speed. By this we mean the speed at which the engine runs most sweetly. It usually lies somewhere between 25 and 30 miles an hour. The rider should find out what this speed is in the case of his own mount, and drive most frequently at that speed. If a long life is desired of an engine it should always be driven well within its maximum capacity, that is to say, on not more than three-quarter throttle, and the engine should not be violently accelerated and decelerated. There is seldom need for this, and it is abuse of an engine in its worst form. Tremendous stresses are thrown upon the whole of the transmission as well as the engine, and cause wear out of all proportion to that caused by moderate handling. If the long life of an engine is desired it should be run in the main with about one-third throttle opening. An engine so handled would always be well within its capabilities.

Use of the Gear-box. The function of the gear-box is to provide variations between the speeds of the engine and rear wheel. Motor-cycles are fitted with a two-, three-, or four-speed gear-box. In bottom gear, the number of revolutions of the engine to each revolution of the back wheel is greater than in top gear, which is the reason why on steep hills one changes to a lower gear to enable the engine revolutions to be maintained, whilst actually the road speed of the machine is less. The gear lever should never be moved unless the clutch lever has been lifted. In the case of some old machines on which a clutch was not fitted, changing gear was usually accomplished by lifting the release valve when moving the gear lever from bottom to top, but when changing down from top to bottom it is better not to lift the release valve, but to let the engine gain speed momentarily before the engagement of the lower gear.

Do not " race " the engine when the machine is standing in neutral, nor keep the machine running for long periods in bottom gear, as this will only cause overheating, and can never serve any useful purpose. On steep hills always change down to a lower gear before the engine begins to labour.

HOW TO HANDLE THE VILLIERS ENGINE 41

Ignition Control. When an engine is provided with variable ignition, it should normally be run with the ignition lever advanced as far as possible consistent with even firing. If a machine is idling on the stand, or pulling slowly through traffic, or heavily laden on a hill, the ignition lever should be retarded a little.

Fitting a Sidecar. It is not recommended, as previously mentioned in Chapter I, to attach a sidecar to a motor-cycle with a Villiers engine smaller than the $3\frac{1}{2}$ h.p. model. This engine has really been designed for sidecar work, and is particularly suitable because of its extraordinary pulling powers. If the machine has previously been used for solo work, it is, of course, necessary to lower the gear ratio when a sidecar is added by changing the sprocket on the engine shaft for one with fewer teeth.

There are many combinations in use powered by the Mark 6 E and Mark 8 E (197 c.c.) engines. The engines are to standard specification but it is usual for the manufacturers to fit a larger rear-wheel sprocket in order to give a lower overall gear ratio.

Noises and their Significance. Mechanically a two-stroke engine is very quiet, because it has no timing gears, tappets, or valves, which even in the best designed four-stroke engine create a certain amount of noise. On two-stroke engines the only normal sounds are a slight " hiss " at the air intake of the carburettor, and the regular " purr " of the exhaust, and even this is less offensive to the ear than the exhaust of a four-stroke, because of its greater frequency and consequently closer approach to a musical note. Should any foreign sound make itself evident immediate investigation should be made, because it will denote an irregularity somewhere.

Various troubles in an engine have their own particular noise, and should one become evident it is best to let the manufacturers, or a recognized Villiers service agent, inspect the machine. If at any time the usually healthy sound of the exhaust becomes " muffled " it indicates that the silencer and exhaust pipes require cleaning internally, because a thick coating of carbon has accumulated and is causing back pressure. When the engine itself begins to run harshly it is usually a sign that it needs decarbonizing.

Four-stroking. This is a fault from which present-day two-stroke engines do not often suffer, although, unfortunately, many of the older engines were rather prone to do so. It is nothing serious, nor is it in any way detrimental to the engine. It indicates usually that the mixture supplied by the carburettor is too rich, so rich in fact, that it will not always ignite, with the result that combustion does not occur every revolution, but only irregularly. Four-stroking can be cured by weakening slightly the mixture, and by keeping the engine running under load. The trouble almost invariably manifests itself at low speeds.

Another cause of four-stroking and irregular running is due to over-oiling. This is always indicated by an excessive amount of blue smoke from the exhaust pipe and can of course be cured by reducing the oil supply.

Coasting. When descending normal main road hills, no special precautions need be taken, but on very steep by-lanes it is sometimes advisable not to descend in top gear, but to engage a lower one, because then the rider has greater control over his machine. Remember that on a two-stroke engine a most powerful brake is the release valve, and this can be used whenever required without any detriment.

Engine Troubles. All petrol engines are susceptible to troubles of various nature, but usually the greater part is of a minor character and can generally be traced to some neglect or oversight on the rider's part. Engine trouble results in one of three things : (*a*) refusal to start, (*b*) indifferent running, (*c*) complete stoppage. The charts on pages 43, 44, and 45 should prove useful to those Villiers riders who lack the experience necessary to diagnose immediately any cause of engine failure.

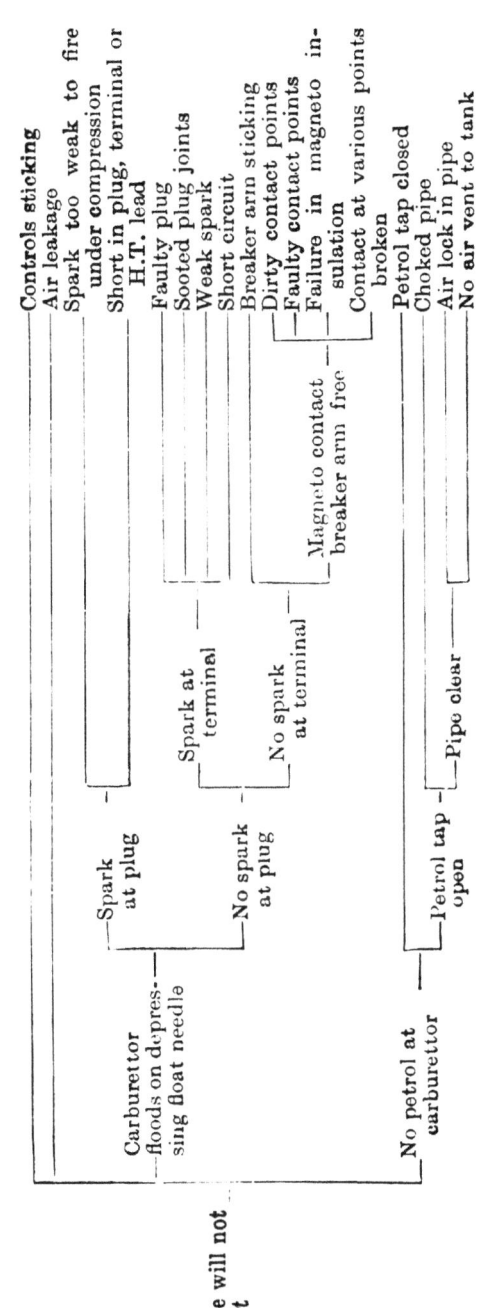

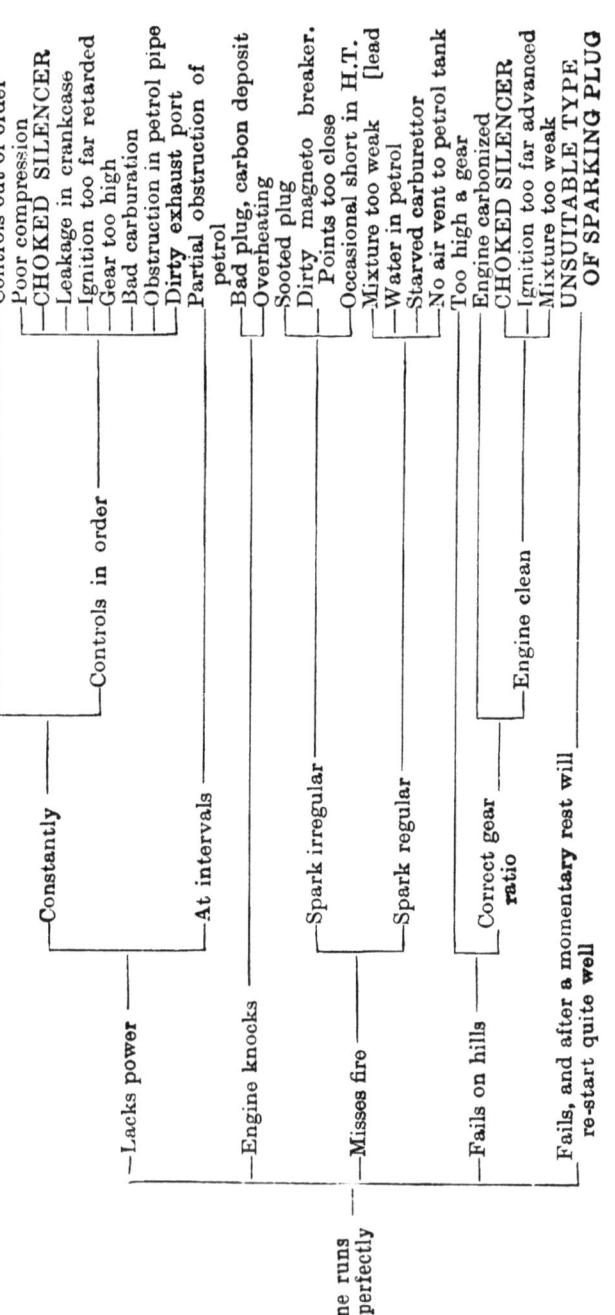

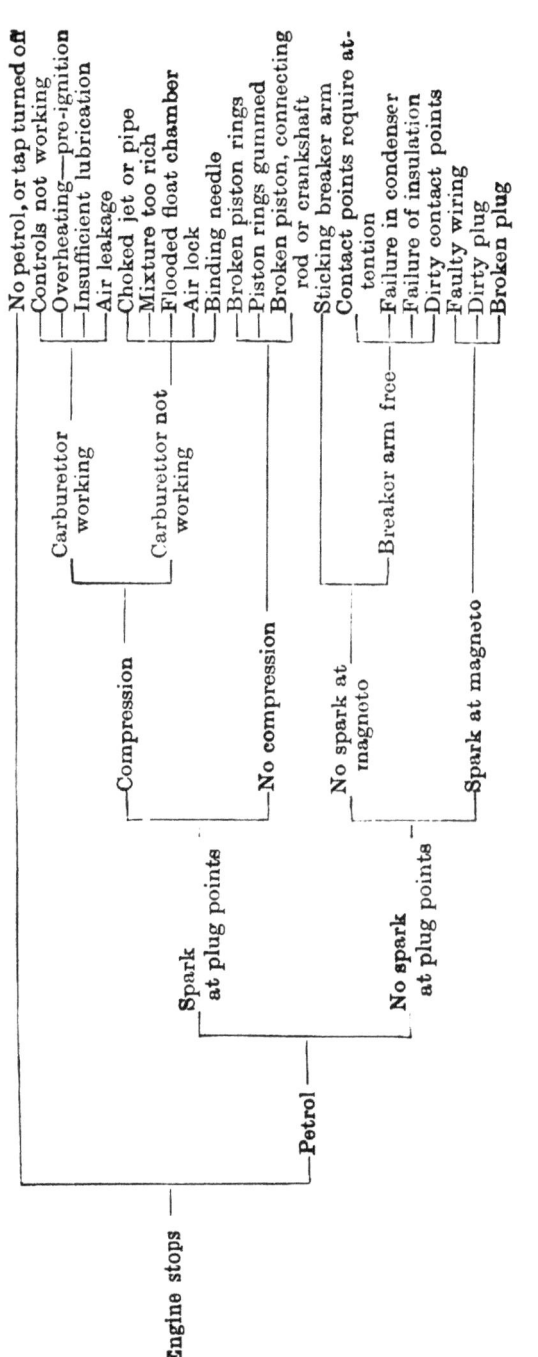

CHAPTER V

OVERHAULING

MOST owners of Villiers engined motor-cycles may desire to overhaul their engines when it becomes necessary, which time varies according to the mileage and the condition of usage. A complete overhaul is generally advisable after every 8,000 miles, and it is then worth while dismantling the engine completely and inspecting the components for wear and making such replacements as are deemed necessary.

Apart from this complete overhaul which most riders make annually, it is advisable to undertake a minor overhaul every 2,000 miles. This comprises: decarbonization of the engine, a superficial examination, and a general checking over of nuts for tightness. The following notes should enable all Villiers engine owners to overhaul their engines with little or no difficulty.

The Tool Kit. Complete overhauls of Villiers engines can be performed with only a small number of tools additional to those included in the standard kit supplied with the machine. They should include a hammer, a long screwdriver, a good adjustable spanner, such as the Lucas girder wrench, and, if possible, a small vice. The latter, while not essential, is a very desirable article in a garage where overhauling work is undertaken. The Villiers Engineering Company supply three excellent spanners (Fig. 30) known as: the "Hammer-tight" spanner which is suitable for the crankshaft and flywheel nuts, a plug spanner for easy removal of the plug, and a magneto spanner fitted with a feeler gauge for the correct adjustment of the contact-breaker points.

Cleaning the Engine. Before commencing to take down an engine, it is always advisable to clean it thoroughly externally if dirty. Dirt is the enemy of accurate adjustments, and, besides hiding defects, renders doubly difficult the task of overhauling. Moreover, as the work of dismantling proceeds, accumulated filth, if not removed, is liable to find its way into the crankcase and bearings, from which it is very difficult to eradicate. Paraffin and a stiff brush should be used for cleaning the engine exterior. This may occupy some considerable time, but it cannot reasonably be neglected. And here we would point out the desirability of having in the garage a good-size tray containing paraffin. As the engine components are removed they should be placed in

OVERHAULING

this and properly cleaned, afterwards being wiped dry with a rag free from fluff. They should then be placed in a methodical order on a white piece of paper until they are required for re-assembling. This procedure may sound somewhat unnecessary, but in actual practice it is found that a great amount of time and trouble is spared thereby. All experienced mechanics will vouch for this statement.

DISMANTLING

Removing Carburettor, Release Valve, Petrol Pipes, etc. Preliminary to removing the cylinder for decarbonization (and this

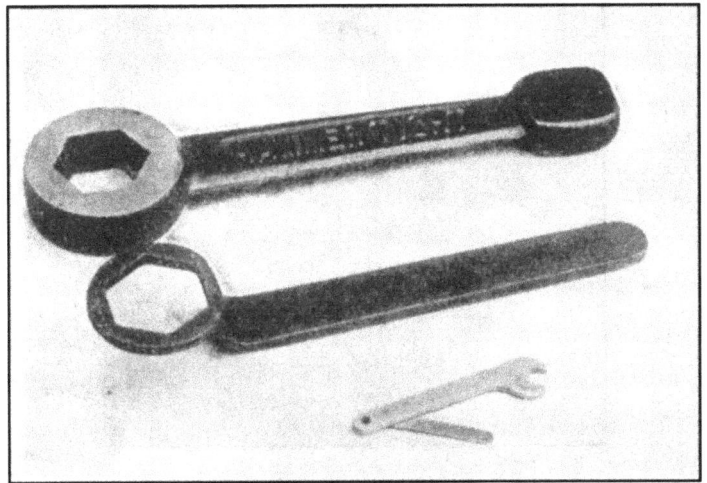

FIG. 30. SHOWING THE SPECIAL VILLIERS SPANNERS AND 0·015 FEELER GAUGE

is advisable even though detachable heads are provided), it is necessary to take off the carburettor and all other fittings liable to obstruct and hinder the removal of the cylinder itself. Firstly, disconnect the petrol pipe unions after seeing that the tap is turned off, taking great care not to use more violence than is necessary. The pipes are easily twisted, and their soldered unions readily tear asunder. Therefore, never undo the union nuts with a large wrench. Having disconnected the petrol pipes, remove the carburettor itself. Now disconnect the terminal at the sparking plug, and unscrew the latter, taking care not to lose the copper and asbestos washer. Also remove the release valve. Then proceed to remove the exhaust pipe, or pipes. The cylinder is now ready for removal.

Cylinder Removal. In the case of engines with detachable heads, undo the bolts holding the cylinder head on to the cylinder barrel, and gently prise the head off with a screwdriver. When doing this slacken the bolts off uniformly by working diagonally. Care should be taken to prise upwards only, to avoid damaging the fin immediately below, which is rather fragile. Having removed the head (see Fig. 24), unscrew the four nuts at the cylinder base which retain the barrel in position, and then after turning the crankshaft round until the piston is at its lowest position gently draw off the barrel but do not twist it round the

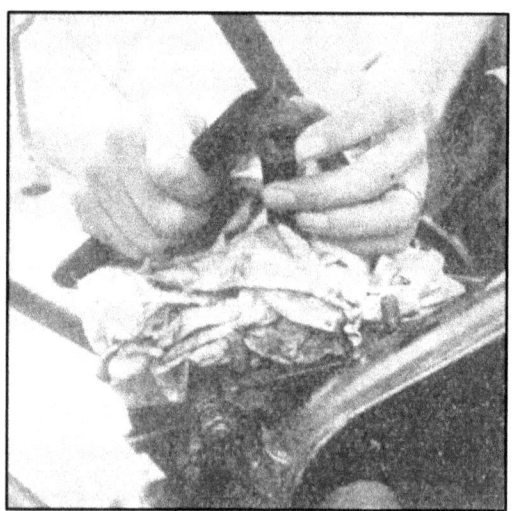

Fig. 31. Covering up the Crankcase to Prevent Dirt Falling Inside

piston as one of the rings may catch on a port. Do not allow the piston to fall sharply against the connecting rod, as this may cause a breakage. Similarly avoid letting the connecting rod strike the edge of the crankcase. Immediately after removing the cylinder wrap a rag around the lower part of the connecting rod in such a way that the hole exposing the crankcase interior is entirely covered up (see Fig. 31). If this is not done there is great danger of dirt and even bolts and nuts being dropped within, which would necessitate taking the crankcase apart. Now remove the piston.

Removing the Piston. To do this with the floating gudgeon pin type simply press out the gudgeon pin with the finger, noting the direction in which it is taken out, so that it may be replaced in exactly the same manner. And here it is well to emphasize the fact that it is desirable to replace all engine components exactly in the same position previous to dismantling, even though they may be of the same design, and, perhaps, nominally interchangeable.

On the earlier type Villiers engines the gudgeon pin was not fully floating, but was a driving fit in the piston bosses, which were very slightly tapered. When in position it was prevented from moving endwise by split pins at either side (see Fig. 25).

To prevent the gudgeon pin being driven in or out from the wrong side, the piston is marked " drive in " and " drive out." Before attempting to remove the gudgeon pin, the split pin on the

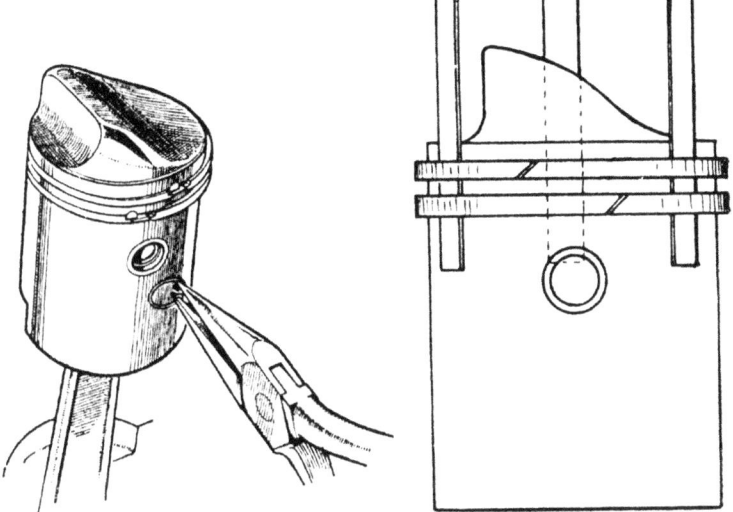

FIG. 32A. REMOVING A CIRCLIP TO RELEASE THE GUDGEON PIN
(*From " The Motor Cycle," London*)

FIG. 32B. HOW TO REMOVE PISTON RINGS WITHOUT DAMAGE

side marked " drive out " must be taken away with a pair of pliers. The gudgeon pin can then be tapped out of position by means of a small piece of brass, or copper, a little smaller in diameter than the gudgeon pin itself. Carefully support the opposite side of the piston by hand to avoid straining the connecting rod. When replacing the gudgeon pin the same method should be employed, but, of course, it will be driven into the piston on the opposite side to that from which it was driven out. When replacing, the small split pin must again be put into position, and the ends of the split pin opened out to prevent it coming adrift. Where a floating gudgeon pin is used as in the later models, aluminium pads are fitted in each end to prevent cylinder-wall damage. When cold these pins are a push-fit in the pistons.

In the 98 c.c. Junior, the 122 c.c. Mark 9 D, the 249 c.c. Mark

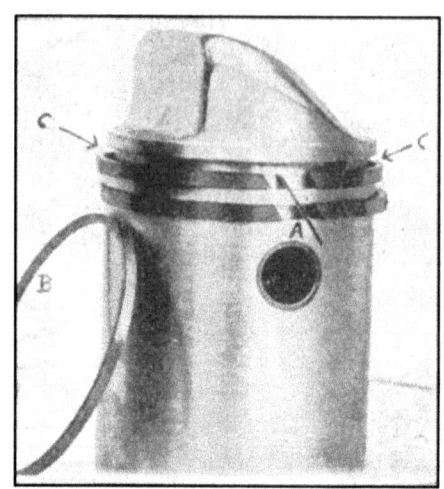

FIG. 33. THE INERTIA RING
A the key, *B* the inertia ring,
C the inertia ring groove

FIG. 34. MARKS WHICH INDICATE
BADLY FITTING PISTON RINGS

XVIII A engines, and others with flat-topped pistons the gudgeon pin is held in place by a circlip, that in one end only of the pin being removed by grasping the protruding ears with a pair of pointed pliers (see Fig. 32A). The gudgeon pin is then pushed out with a strip of wood. When refitting, new circlips should always be used. A damaged clip may cause trouble.

Should there be brown or black marks on the piston, as shown clearly in Fig. 34, it may denote that the burned gases are blowing past, and may be due to the piston rings being badly worn, or stuck in their grooves. A piston very loose in the cylinder bore indicates the need for regrinding the cylinder, and fitting oversize piston and rings. This should be done by the manufacturers, who have standard limits for such work. It is a waste of time fitting new rings in an endeavour to compensate for an enlarged cylinder bore, due to wear.

Piston Rings. These are of cast iron, and being of very small section must be handled very, very carefully. If not, they will certainly be broken. They cannot safely be opened out wider than will allow them to slip over the crown of the piston. Therefore, to put them on or remove them requires the insertion of small strips of thin metal about $\frac{1}{4}$ in. wide, which are placed in the manner illustrated by Fig. 32B.

The inertia ring fitted to the latest type pistons should not be taken off, for if strained in any way the ends may foul the ports.

The piston rings are the main guard of the compression. They must, therefore, be full of spring and free in their grooves. If all the rings are bright all the way round, they are obviously being polished against the cylinder walls, and are perfect, and should be left alone. If, on the other hand, they are dull or stained at some points, they are not in proper contact with the walls of the cylinder. Perhaps they are stuck in their grooves with burnt oil, and will function properly if the grooves are cleaned. If vertically loose in their grooves and very badly marked, the rings must be renewed. The rings must make a perfectly gas-tight joint the whole way round the piston. In Fig. 35 we have an example of distortion as shown by the brownish marks to the right. This points to the fact that gas is escaping past the rings at these darkened areas.

Where no inertia ring is fitted, the rings are anchored with pegs in the grooves to stop rings working round. Care must be taken therefore to replace the rings the proper way up and to work them round so that the gaps coincide with the pegs.

In those engines where an inertia ring is used, the piston rings are secured by a key fitted across the grooves.

When fitting new rings be quite sure to test them in the cylinder by pushing them a little way down with the skirt of the piston. In this way you can get the rings quite square in the barrel, and then the gaps in the rings, if of the peg type, if all is correct, should be approximately six-thousandths or eight-thousandths of an inch (0·006 in. or 0·008 in.). With later models, allowance has to be made for the key, and the gap will be approximately 0·045 to 0·050 in. If the gap is less than this the rings will be

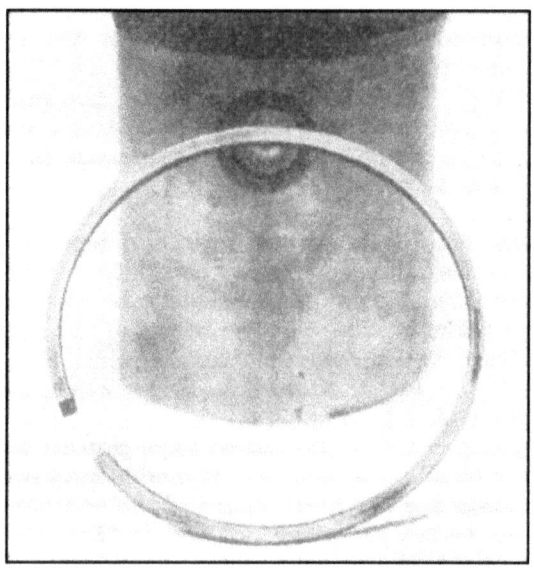

FIG. 35. MARKS INDICATING DISTORTED RINGS

too tight when the engine is warm, and, therefore, a small amount should be filed away very carefully from the edges of the gap (after taking the piston ring out of the cylinder) to enable it to close further.

If, in the case of a used piston ring, it has worn to such an extent that the gap exceeds one-thirty-second of an inch the ring should be replaced.

Removal of Carbon. The formation of carbon is caused through incomplete burning of the fuel and oil, and a very heavy deposit of carbon will generally indicate that the engine has been overoiled excessively. A certain amount of road dust and foreign matter which finds its way into the engine will also form a part of this carbon, and a very hard formation is usually the result

OVERHAULING

of using too rich a fuel mixture. The presence of carbon in an engine causes rough running and harshness, due to the fact that it lessens the available space for combustion, and as a consequence increases the compression ratio. The above will serve to explain why it is necessary periodically to decarbonize an engine, and the best way of doing this is described in the following pages.

HOW TO DECARBONIZE

The Cylinder and Piston. If the engine has a detachable head this should be removed first, and, for what is known as a " top

FIG. 36 THE PEGS WHICH PREVENT PISTON RINGS ROTATING ON A TWO-STROKE

overhaul," it will not be necessary to take off the cylinder barrel, because the removal of the head itself will also expose the top of the piston and enable that to be cleaned. As previously mentioned in this book, however, it is essential occasionally to remove the complete cylinder barrel, so that the inside of the piston may also receive attention. Whenever the cylinder barrel is removed, a piece of clean rag should be stuffed into the top of the crankcase round the projecting connecting rod, to prevent dirt and even small parts falling into the crankcase. This is an important precaution, and should always be observed as it often saves considerable trouble, and may prevent serious damage, especially if a part falls into the crankcase unobserved.

Having removed the cylinder head the carbon should be carefully chipped and scraped out by means of a blunt instrument,

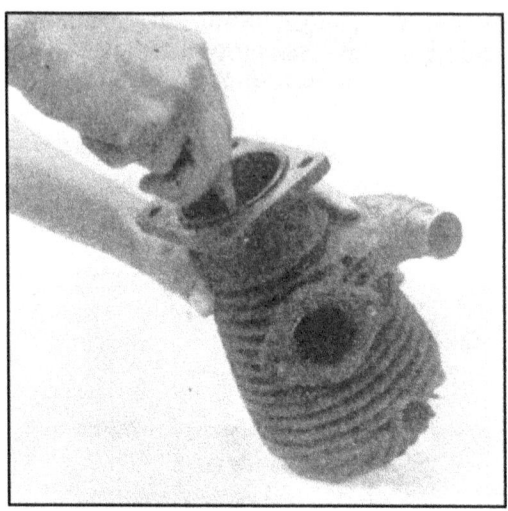

Fig. 37. Decarbonizing a Cylinder

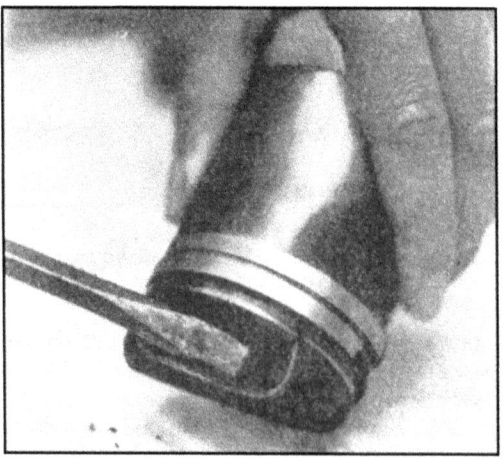

Fig. 38. Cleaning the Piston Head

such as a screwdriver. (See Fig. 37.) Never use a sharp-edged tool which would cut into the aluminium.

Having removed the thick carbon, take a piece of fine emery cloth and polish the inside of the head with a circular movement, afterwards cleaning it thoroughly with a paraffin-soaked rag to remove all traces of loose emery and carbon. The paraffin rag will also help to add a polish to the metal if the emery cloth was sufficiently fine and used thoroughly. In the case of a cast-iron cylinder integral with its head, a screwdriver long enough to reach right down inside the barrel to the head must be used, and the carbon chipped out with it. This chipping can be done with a little more force than is possible in the case of the aluminium

FIG. 39. REMOVING CARBON FROM INSIDE A PISTON

cylinder head, because, of course, iron is much harder, and is, therefore, not so easily damaged. The operation will probably take a little longer to do because it is a little more inaccessible, but owing to the symmetry of a two-stroke cylinder head it is far easier to decarbonize than, for instance, a side-valve, four-stroke cylinder head.

The cylinder head can be polished to quite a bright finish by means of a piece of emery cloth on the end of the screwdriver, if care and a little patience is exercised.

More efficient results are obtained from a smooth surface in the combustion chamber, because if any little lumps of carbon or metal are left projecting they are liable to become incandescent and cause pre-ignition.

The piston top must now receive attention, and should be scraped free from carbon with the same screwdriver or similar tool, taking great care, especially in the case of an aluminium piston, not to damage the surface of the metal. The piston top should then be polished with very fine emery cloth until it is free from every black trace of carbon. If the cylinder barrel has been removed, the piston should be taken off its connecting rod, and the inside of its head chipped free of carbon, as shown in Fig. 39. When dealing with the piston, care should be taken in handling it, because the sides are very thin. Also remove all carbon from gudgeon pin and piston bosses.

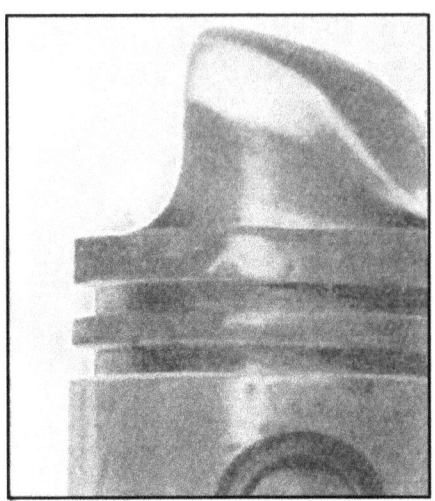

FIG. 40. CLEAN THE PISTON RING GROOVES BEFORE REPLACING RINGS

Piston Ring Grooves. The piston rings should next be taken off (see Fig. 40), and the grooves carefully scraped free of carbon, and made quite clean by rubbing round them a small piece of rag soaked in paraffin. Whilst doing this, it is advisable to get someone to hold the piston, rather than to put it in a vice.

Cylinder Ports. These should next receive attention, the exhaust port in particular, and all traces of carbon removed from them. The sides of the ports should be afterwards polished with emery cloth, but under no circumstances should they be filed, because, if their slightly irregular shape is made quite square, the timing of the engine will be affected.

(IMPORTANT. See the paragraph on Silencers, page 61.)

The Cylinder Exterior. In the course of many miles a certain amount of oil is almost bound to be thrown on to the outside of the cylinder, and mud will cling to this oil and result in time in a thick coating on the fins, rendering them more or less inefficient as heat dissipators. This deposit should, therefore, be removed

OVERHAULING

(see Fig. 42), and then the cylinder should be cleaned with paraffin and a stiff brush. Afterwards, if any score is set by appearance, the cylinder can be repainted with one of the special black preparations on the market to restore its previously neat appearance.

EXAMINATION FOR WEAR, AND REASSEMBLY

Release Valve. In course of time, the seating of this valve will become damaged by heat, and also by small particles of carbon lodging on its face and making the seat irregular.

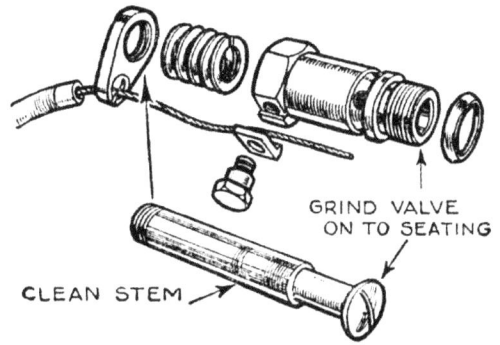

Fig. 41. How to Deal with the Villiers Release Valve after it has been Removed and Dismantled
(*From "The Motor Cycle," London*)

The release valve must be perfectly gas-tight. The points to note are: (1) proper and clean seating of the valve, (2) that the fitting is screwed into the cylinder head on to a good sound copper washer, and (3) that the adjustment of the control lever and wire allows for the full action of the spring to return the valve to its seating. (Fig. 41.)

A proper overhaul cannot be given unless the whole component is removed. A vigorous brushing with paraffin will clean it of its grime. The valve and its seating should be examined, and, if badly marked, must be " ground " in. A fine valve-grinding paste or mixture of emery and paraffin is applied to the valve seating, and the valve rotated (in half turns) by means of a screwdriver in the slot in the valve head, until the grinding action of the paste produces clean, even, and level surfaces. It must then be swilled thoroughly with paraffin. See that the washer is in good condition—better still renew. The valve return spring should be lively, but if it has been softened by heat, fit a new one.

The adjustment of the control cable is simple on Villiers engines. The wire is merely threaded through a hole at the top of the

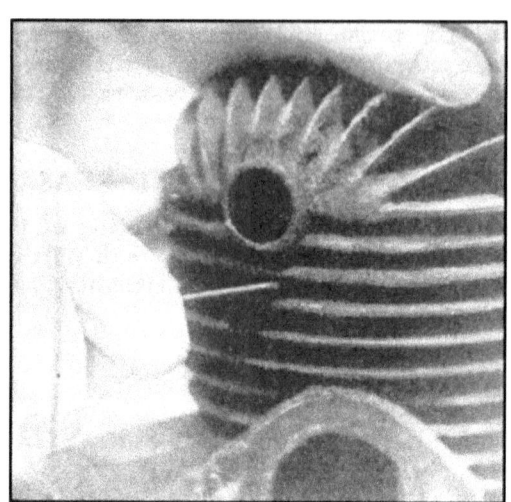

Fig. 42. Removing Accumulated Oil from the Cylinder Exterior

Fig. 43. Applying Cylinder Black after Cleaning

OVERHAULING

body, and when the proper adjustment is made, is locked by screwing down a set-screw. When reassembling the release valve, see that the cable is adjusted to have the minimum amount of slack.

A Worn Cylinder. After much use a cylinder bore tends to become slightly oval because wear is greater across the thrust faces than at points diametrically at right angles to them. Bore wear is also greatest at the top of the cylinder, the point of maximum wear coinciding approximately with the upper limit

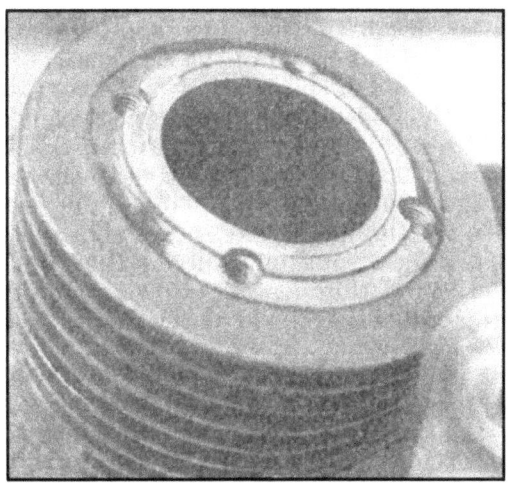

Fig. 44. Make Sure the Cylinder Barrel Top Faces are Clean Before Replacing Head

of piston-ring travel. Eventually the cylinder bore becomes so large that the engine is inefficient. This is time for the cylinder to be re-bored, and an oversize piston and rings fitted. It is a waste of time to fit oversize rings on to a standard piston in a worn bore in an endeavour temporarily to effect an improvement. Re-boring will be a permanent job, and this work should always be done by the makers of the engine, who work to fixed dimensions and have recognized limits for these parts. When returned by them the cylinder and piston will fit as on a brand new engine, and, consequently, the engine should again carefully be run in as when new.

Do not let inexperienced people re-bore your cylinder because, in nine cases out of ten, they cannot do this satisfactorily.

Reassembling. Prior to this, make sure that the oilways in the crankcase and cylinder are clear. It is best to squirt paraffin through them by means of a syringe, so that no oil or dirt can lodge in them and cause a shortage of oil. Washers and joints should be renewed before the parts are replaced. This applies particularly to the induction manifold washer (if a separate inlet pipe is fitted to your model) and to the cylinder-base washer.

It is advisable to purchase a new cylinder-base washer from the makers, so that the holes are cut to correspond with the oilways. Fitting a home-made washer may have disastrous results.

Swill out the crankcase with paraffin before refitting the cylinder, spin the crankshaft round by pressing the connecting rod up and down to splash the paraffin about, and then drain off through the plug in the bottom of the crankcase.

The piston can now be replaced, but make sure that it is fitted correctly. With the deflector-head piston the sloping side of the deflector should face forward, and the short vertical side should point to the rear. The rings are best fitted to the piston before it is placed on the connecting rod. Make quite sure the gaps correspond with the ring pegs or keys on the piston before replacing the cylinder. Smear some oil thinly on the cylinder walls with the fingers, and also a thin coating on the piston itself. Do not pour oil into the crankcase which, at the most, should contain *no more than a teaspoonful.*

The cylinder should be held in the right hand with the exhaust ports pointing forward ; turn the crankshaft so that the piston is at its lowest position, and then hold the latter with the left hand, squeezing the rings as they are slipped into the bore of the cylinder. Push the cylinder down straight ; do not twist from side to side, otherwise a ring may catch in one of the ports, and it will then in all probability have to be broken before the cylinder can be moved. If your cylinder has a detachable head, fit this afterwards, and not before replacing the barrel. There should be no gasket or washer between the barrel and cylinder head. Nor should any jointing compound be employed, as this tends to insulate the two parts of the cylinder, and prevent proper dissipation of the heat from the barrel. A gas-tight joint is made quite satisfactorily by the hard iron of the barrel biting into the softer aluminium of the head.

After replacing the barrel, screw on the holding-down nuts and spring washers, tightening each of them down in order by half a turn at a time as they become tight. The cylinder head bolts should be tightened similarly. Screw these nuts and head bolts as tight as possible, and then, when the engine has subsequently been run for a short while, it will be found possible to tighten them still further, but this must be done evenly.

Exhaust Pipes and Silencers. Attention to these parts is probably the most important of all, and many strange disappearances of power in a two-stroke engine are attributable to these components. A thick coating of soot will form inside the exhaust pipes, which must be thoroughly cleaned, and the same attention should be paid to the silencer. It is impossible to give details of the procedure to be adopted in every case, because most machines have a different type of silencer, according to the manufacturer's own design, but it must be taken as a general rule that these must be kept clear and free from carbon.

If a silencer, with internal baffle plates having small holes drilled in them is employed, the carbon will tend to form on the edges of these holes and close them in, resulting in time in only a very small aperture through which the gases may escape. This must be corrected. If the silencer has a filling, as in some cases, of a bundle of metal turnings, the soot will adhere to this in a remarkable manner, and it is almost impossible to remove. In such a case it is advisable to replace with a new filling, or omit altogether, but in the latter case the machine may be too noisy.

A flue brush is a very useful thing for putting down long exhaust pipes to clean from soot. In an old machine, to which probably no attention has been paid for a long time to the exhaust pipes, the carbon may be very hard to remove, and the only way to treat it then is to get the pipe or silencer hot in a fire, and then tap on the outside to loosen the carbon. This will, of course, destroy any enamel or plating on the outside, but it is certainly worth while from the point of view of increased efficiency obtained. The silencer can always be re-enamelled afterwards.

Chains and Chain Sprockets. The engine sprocket should be examined. After much use the teeth may assume a hooked formation through wear, in which case the sprocket should be replaced because it will have a damaging result on the chain.

The primary chain, i.e. the one from the engine to the gear-box, as it runs at a very high speed, will wear more rapidly than the final driving chain. The rollers should be carefully examined to make sure that none are missing, and the chain should be tested for stretch and play by laying it straight along the bench and holding the two ends to see by how much the chain can be deflected sideways. If the chain will bend considerably, it indicates that it is rather badly worn, and will be noisy in use, and, owing to the fact that some links will be stretched more than others, it will be impossible to get an even tension on the whole of its length, with the result that in some positions it will be tight, and in others it will be loose enough to rattle against the chain cover. It is, therefore, advisable to replace it.

Bushes and Bearings. The various components noted upon for examination and attention apply to a top overhaul. In a general overhaul and examination, the engine should really be taken from the frame and then dismantled completely, but before taking the crankcase apart the shaft bearings should receive examination. Badly worn bearings will cause noise and inefficient running, and if neglected will become rapidly worse. After removing the cylinder and piston, the engine should be held in a vice by means

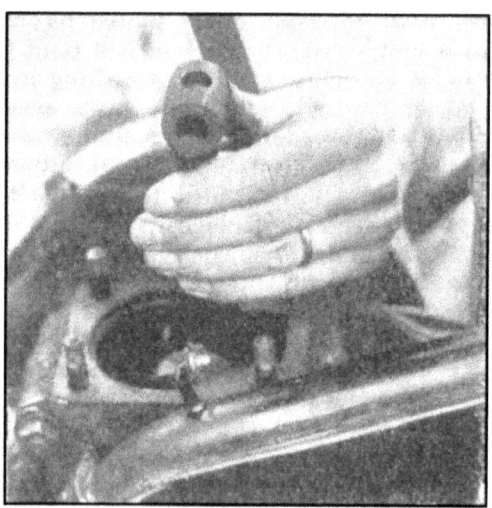

FIG. 45. TESTING FOR PLAY IN THE BIG-END BEARINGS

of one of the crankcase bolt lugs. The crankcase main bearings can be tested by gripping the sprocket on the shaft, and lifting it up and down to see if any play exists between the shaft and its bushes. A certain amount of end play will be noticed when doing this, and this must not be confused with up and down play. End play is essential in an engine, and although it may apparently be considerable, actual measurements will show that it is only a few thousandths of an inch, and may be ignored altogether. Actually, there should be no discernible up-and-down movement, and if there is, it is advisable to have the bushes replaced by new ones. This work is best carried out by the manufacturers, who have tools and machinery for extracting old bushes and fitting new ones without distorting or damaging the crankcase, and the new bearings, which are always slightly contracted when being pressed into the crankcase, can be bored out by the manufacturers to the correct size for the shafts.

OVERHAULING

It is rare for these bushes to require replacement, and it is very unusual for any Villiers engine, having done less than 20,000 miles, to require new main bushes. The big-end bearing in the connecting rod also should not require replacement or attention in less than that mileage, but it is just as well to test this when the engine is dismantled. The condition of this bearing is best ascertained by gripping the connecting rod with the hand, as shown in Fig. 45, when the crankshaft is at the top of its stroke, and seeing whether any up-and-down movement can be detected. It will be found

FIG. 46. A CRANKCASE HALF
This must be quite clean and a new washer fitted before reassembly

possible to move the connecting rod from side to side, but this is essential, and does not indicate that any wear has taken place in the bearing itself.

If the crankcase is taken apart in order that the shafts may be removed, the best way of doing this after removing the bolts is to tap the crankcase lightly with a wooden mallet. Never prise the two halves apart with a screwdriver.

When reassembling the crankcase always fit a new paper washer, and this may be smeared lightly with adhesive to improve the joint. It is not advisable for the owner to take his crankshaft apart, but should it be found necessary to replace rollers at any time in the big-end bearing, let the manufacturers replace them. The only other bearing is the small-end of the connecting rod in which the gudgeon pin oscillates. This can be tested by inserting the gudgeon pin in the small-end, and observing with the fingers what tendency it has to rock up and down. If considerable movement is found here, the wear may have taken place either in the connecting rod bush, or on the gudgeon pin, or both, and the worn part, or parts, should be replaced. Extracting the old bush and fitting a new one in the small-end of the connecting rod can be carried out by the amateur if necessary. The bush should not be driven out by force. It is best to proceed as follows: Obtain an old bush, the outside diameter of which is slightly smaller than that of the one to be extracted, and also another bush, the inside diameter of which is slightly larger than the outside diameter of the original bush. Place these two bushes, one at either side of the small-end, and then run a bolt through the three of them and screw a nut and large washer on to it. By tightening up this nut, the small bush will push the centre one out of the connecting rod into the large bush at the other side. The new small-end bush which is to be fitted can be inserted in a similar manner, but by reversing the above procedure. In doing this care should be taken to see that it is not damaged.

The above remarks have dealt entirely with the Villiers engine. Reference to the maintenance of its fly-wheel magneto, and carburettor, are given in subsequent chapters.

It is impossible here to describe the overhaul of the cycle parts of the machine, because these vary according to the make, and it is best to get details from the manufacturers of the motor-cycle.

In concluding this chapter, it is here, perhaps, as well to mention that spare parts for most Villiers engines, can be obtained. Official stockists of these replacements have been appointed throughout the British Isles, and the name of your nearest dealer will be supplied upon application to the Villiers Engineering Co., Ltd., Wolverhampton. To ensure the correct parts being supplied, always quote the engine number and prefixed letters which are stamped on the crankcase just beneath the cylinder flange. This indicates to the manufacturer or the stockist exactly the type of engine, and thus avoids mistakes.

CHAPTER VI

THE VILLIERS FLY-WHEEL MAGNETO

The Principle of the Magneto. Let us explain first of all how a magneto works. Between the "poles," i.e. the two lower ends of an ordinary magnet, fields of "force" exist. This may be termed simply "magnetic influence." It was found that when a conductor consisting of many turns of wire was rotated between these poles, a current was produced in the coil of wire. This is known as the "primary" coil. Now if another coil of wire is wound round and along this primary coil, but not in electrical contact (i.e. insulated), and if the circuit in the primary coil is broken, a current of high pressure (voltage) is immediately induced in this outside coil (called the "secondary" coil). It is this current that is supplied to the plug and causes the spark at the points. The wires are wound round a core made of soft iron, called an armature.

The diagram (Fig. 47) explains the idea simply. The armature is at A. The heavy lines represent the primary windings, the light lines the secondary windings. E is the condenser (explained below); C the sparking plug; D the armature plate; B the contact breaker.

Let us trace the circuits. The thick line indicates the primary circuit, the light lines the secondary high tension circuits.

The Armature. This is rotated between the poles of a magnet which produces a low tension current in the thick line circuit —flowing to the fixed contact point in the contact breaker where the points are closed, and back by way of the armature plate to the other end of the primary wiring. Immediately this circuit is interrupted, a high pressure current is induced in the outside secondary wirings which is circulated by way of the armature plate to the plug, and back through the engine metal itself.

In the case of the Villiers fly-wheel magneto, the magnet is rotated round the armature and windings which are stationary. Thus the same effect is produced, but with fewer moving parts and less liability of damage to the windings.

The Condenser. This, as will be seen, is placed in the primary circuit "parallel" with the contact breaker. On page 66, its functions are dealt with from a practical point of view only.

It consists of sheets of tinfoil and mica (as an insulator) packed alternately together. When the primary circuit is broken an " extra " current is induced in this same winding which, if there were no condenser, would cause a spark to pass between the contact points in the contact breaker. This would burn them away in a short time. When a condenser is placed in the circuit, the large capacity of the tinfoil surfaces enables the condenser to " take " this current. A further advantage is gained in this way —as the condenser remains connected and in circuit, it now discharges itself and sends the current in a reverse direction through

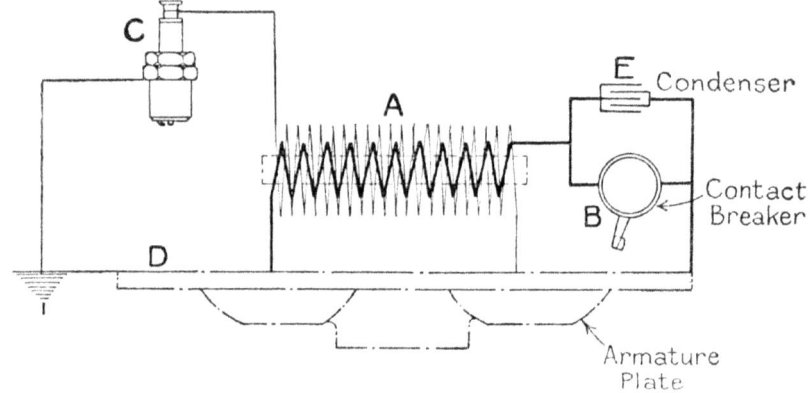

Fig. 47. General Principle of the Magneto

the primary coil, which has the effect of increasing the efficiency and rapidity of the break, and thereby aids in the production of a very high voltage current in the secondary.

The Contact Breaker. As its name signifies, this " breaks contact " in the primary circuit, causing a spark to pass at once between the plug points, due to the high tension current induced in the secondary winding. It consists of one stationary contact point, and one fitted to a lever which is raised and lowered by means of a cam at the other end. This cam in the Villiers magneto rotates with the fly-wheel, and moves the lever (called a rocker arm) at the necessary time when the points are in contact.

Fig. 48 shows the two parts of the Villiers two-pole fly-wheel magneto separated, and the various sections named.

The Advantages and Construction of the Villiers Fly-wheel Magneto. As the name implies, the Villiers magneto is built into the fly-wheel of the machine. This fact alone makes its construction

THE VILLIERS FLY-WHEEL MAGNETO

more simple and, therefore, more easily overhauled and adjusted. It also reduces the weight of the complete engine. There are no platforms necessary to carry it, as with the horseshoe type magneto, and no gears or chains to drive it.

When comparing the actual functioning, several other important advantages will be seen. Firstly, there are no carbon brushes to wear. Secondly, there are no rotating collector rings which are very easily broken, nor delicate bearings requiring lubricant frequently. In fact, the armature itself is stationary—the only movable part being the fly-wheel containing the magnets and

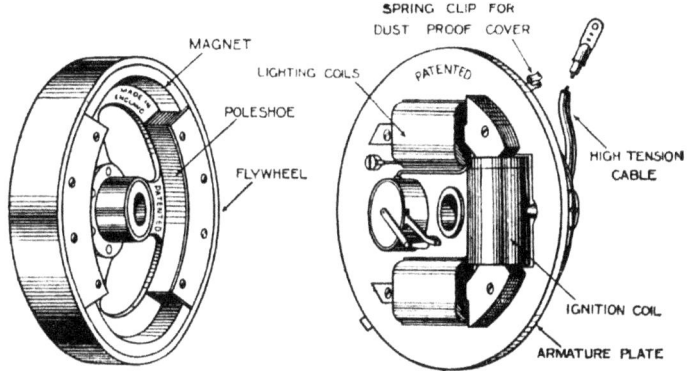

FIG. 48. THE COMPONENT PARTS OF THE VILLIERS 2-POLE FLY-WHEEL MAGNETO

the cam. It is efficiency itself—just a slow turn of the fly-wheel by hand gives an intense spark—and here a most important point is arrived at. It is common to most of the horseshoe type magnetos that the spark becomes weakened when the ignition is retarded. With the Villiers magneto the spark is equally intense in all positions. Again, the amount this magneto can be retarded and advanced is unlimited, but in the horseshoe type the effective range is decidedly limited, and a more efficient coil is obtainable because of the much greater space available. The contact breaker is better protected and less disposed to wear. Undoubtedly, the fly-wheel type magneto has advantages from every point of view. The actual construction is so simple that, by reference to Figs. 48 and 49, the exact position of the various components will be seen. The fly-wheel has three spokes between which the contact breaker can easily be adjusted, and its action may be noted while the engine is working at any speed. Inside the fly-wheel are clamped the magnets, held in position by the pole shoes. A good spark is maintained at very low engine speeds

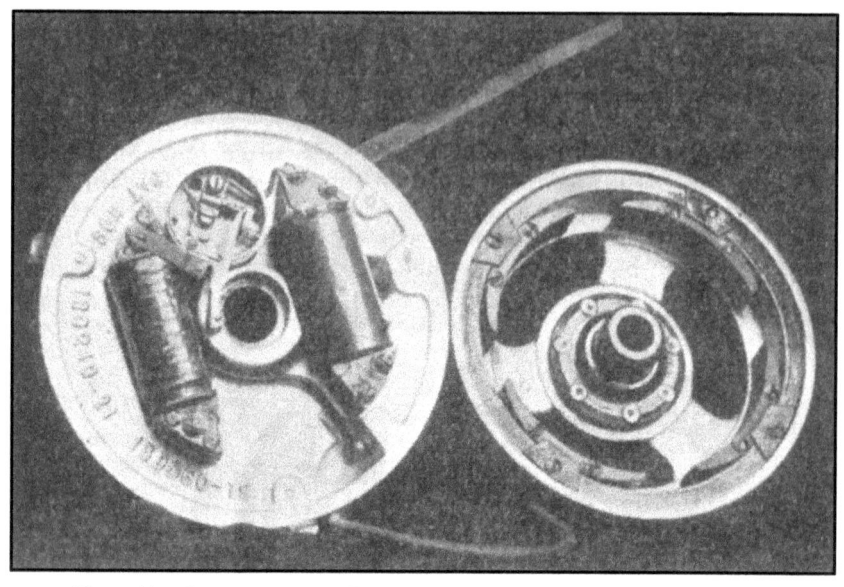

FIG. 49. SHOWING THE VILLIERS 4-POLE FLY-WHEEL MAGNETO

FIG. 50. PLACING A SPANNER ACROSS THE POLE SHOES WHEN THE FLY-WHEEL IS TAKEN DOWN, TO AVOID DEMAGNETIZATION

because the capacity of the magnets in the periphery of the fly-wheel is greater than is possible in other types.

The entire mechanism is kept perfectly clean and dustproof by a cover held in position by spring clips.

Dismantling the Fly-wheel Magneto. Removing the cover will expose the fly-wheel to view, and the latter may be removed by undoing the centre nut. This nut has a flange which draws the fly-wheel from the shaft as it is unscrewed, and this obviates the use of a special extracting tool, and also prevents any damage which might be done to the fly-wheel if it had to be levered from the shaft. As this nut is necessarily very tight, it is advisable not to use an adjustable spanner, the jaws of which are apt to open and damage the corners of the hexagon.

The Villiers Engineering Company supply a special forging known as the "Hammer-tight" spanner at a very reasonable price.

This nut, which has a right-hand thread, is unscrewed in an anti-clockwise direction looking at the face of the fly-wheel. The spanner should be placed on the nut and hammered round in that direction. After about two turns it will be found to tighten. This is because the flange is now pulling against the face of the fly-wheel. If a piece of wood is now placed against the face of the nut and tapped sharply with a hammer it will loosen the fly-wheel on the taper of the shaft, and the nut can be unscrewed with the fingers till the fly-wheel is completely removed. When taken off, a piece of iron, such as a spanner, should be placed across the two pole shoes (see Fig. 50) to prevent the loss of magnetic flux. (Partial demagnetization may occur if the fly-wheel is dropped.) The various components of the armature plate are then readily accessible. It should be noted here that the contact-breaker points are quite accessible without removing the fly-wheel, which should never be taken off unless something more serious requires attention, or if it is necessary to remove the complete magneto for any reason.

The Armature Plate. The armature plate upon most of the older models is held in position by means of a split steel bush, which is contracted to the main engine shaft bush, and a screw regulates the tension of this bush.

In the case of the variable ignition magneto, the screw should be adjusted by means of a long handled screwdriver until just sufficient tension is obtained to allow the armature plate to be moved round by hand, but it should not be sufficiently loose to move by itself. Slackening the screw right off will enable the armature plate to be drawn completely from the engine, but in

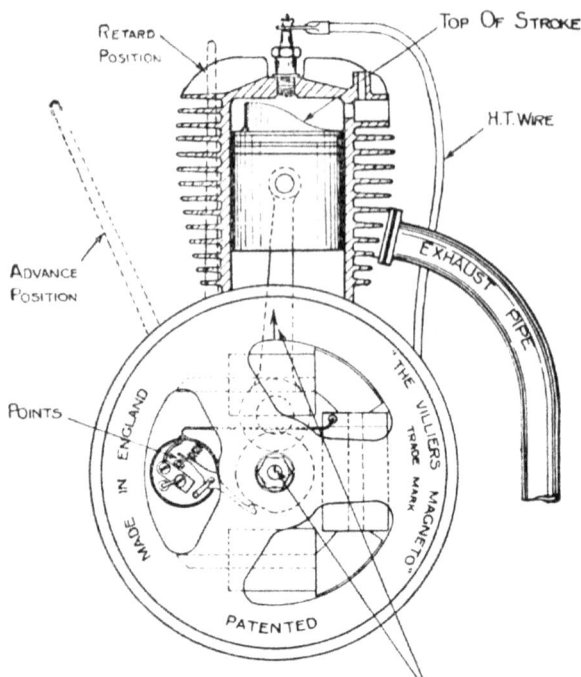

Fig. 51. Diagram Showing how to Retime the Magneto

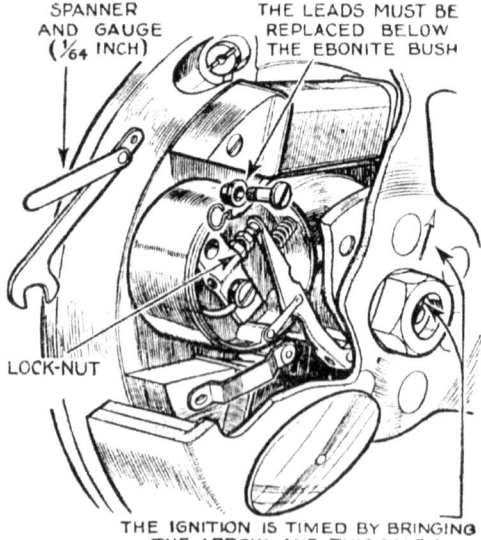

Fig. 52. Points which should Receive Attention in the Fly-wheel Magneto - This drawing also shows how the ignition is timed

THE VILLIERS FLY-WHEEL MAGNETO

the case of the fixed ignition magneto, for instance on the 1¼ h.p. engine, there is a strap connecting the armature plate to one of the crankcase bolts, and this must be removed before the armature plate can be taken off.

Later models have a fixed armature plate held on a spigot on the crankcase with the screws found inside the oil-well in the centre. Variable ignition is thus not possible nor is it necessary.

FIG. 53. THE SPARKING PLUG IN POSITION IN THE VILLIERS CYLINDER HEAD (CUT-AWAY).

FIG. 54. SHOWING THE GAP AT THE SPARKING PLUG POINTS

Refitting the Fly-wheel Magneto. First of all replace the armature plate, and, in the case of the fixed ignition type, position it by means of the strap referred to above. Before fitting the fly-wheel, wipe the taper of the engine shaft, and the corresponding taper inside the cam of the fly-wheel, perfectly clean and dry. Then place the fly-wheel in position and screw up the centre nut. Before the latter is quite tight, set the fly-wheel so that the arrow stamped on its face is in line with, and on the same side of, the centre as the small mark on the end of the engine shaft (see Fig. 51). Hold the fly-wheel in this position and then tighten the centre nut, locking it finally in position by a few sharp blows on the end of the " Hammer-tight " spanner. If this is done accurately, the timing will automatically be correct, because the two marks are so arranged to make the breaking of the contact points coincide with the suitable position of the piston.

In the older models, the lever on the armature plate should be pulled back to the " advance " position, approximately as shown in Fig. 51. When this lever is vertical the ignition is fully retarded.

On current models including the 125 c.c. Unit, the Junior Engine, and the six-pole magnetos there is no manual variation. On these magnetos a line is punched on the rim of the armature plate, near to the high-tension terminal and also

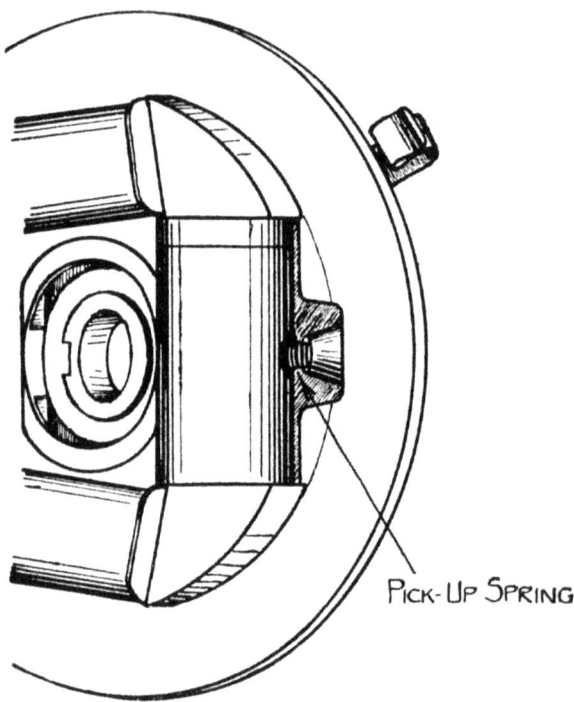

FIG. 55. THIS "PICK-UP" SPRING MUST MAKE CONTACT WITH THE EXPOSED PART OF THE IGNITION COIL

on the fly-wheel rim. To time the magneto, the two lines must be opposite, with the piston at the top of the stroke, the amount of advance being already allowed for when the wheel is marked by the makers.

Adjusting the Contact Points. The accurate adjustment of these points, shown in Fig. 52, is of importance for the efficient running of the engine. Adjustment is only occasionally called for, but this setting will often make all the difference between poor results and a good performance. In the latest improved type of

THE VILLIERS FLY-WHEEL MAGNETO

assembly, adjustment is made with a screwdriver only by unscrewing *A* (with the points fully open), positioning bracket *B* with a 0·015 in. feeler gauge and then tightening up. Screw *C* is not touched (Fig. 56). In the older models two spanners are desirable—one to hold each of the nuts on the adjustable point.

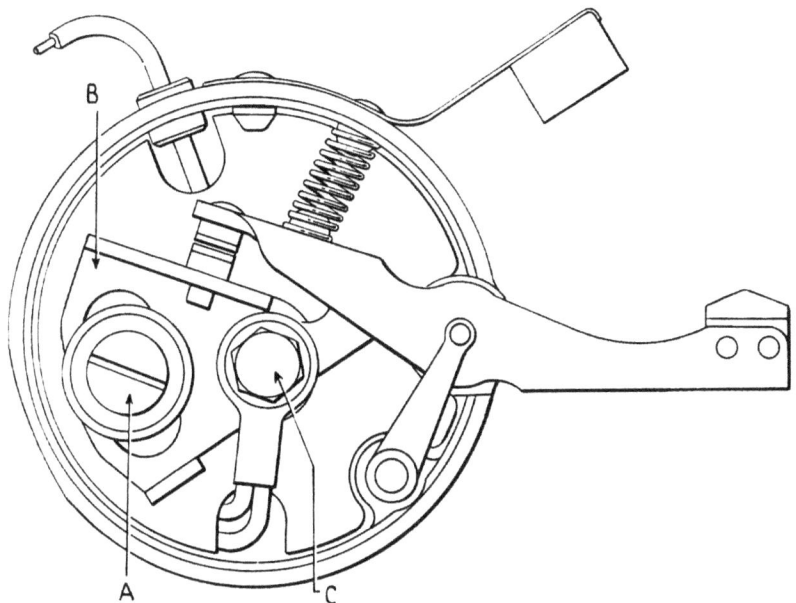

FIG. 56. ADJUSTING THE CONTACT-BREAKER POINTS

First of all, the fly-wheel should be turned round so that the rocker arm is lifted to its highest position on the cam. Then the lock nut (bottom one) should be loosened, and the other nut turned until the faces of the contact points are exactly $\frac{1}{64}$ in. apart. The screwed point should be carefully held in this position while the lock nut is then tightened securely. For accurate setting it is as well to obtain what is known as a "feeler" gauge (see Fig. 30). If the points are set too close, the symptoms are, first of all irregular running and difficult starting. If the points make almost continual contact, starting will be almost impossible, or spasmodic backfiring in the silencer will occur. It is wise to keep the contact points quite clean, and they should occasionally be wiped with a petrol-soaked rag to remove any dust or foreign matter which may collect. Do not ever file the contact points.

Retarded Ignition. Often obscure engine troubles may be traced to a loose armature plate which may cause the adjustment of the points to vary, and may result also in the ignition automatically retarding itself. Such an occurrence will make the engine run hot and in an erratic manner. The remedy is to tighten the armature plate screw referred to above.

Ignition troubles are rare ; if, for instance, difficulty is experienced in starting the engine, investigations should first be made to ascertain that the engine is receiving a supply of petrol. Press the "tickler" on the carburettor, and if petrol flows that may be taken as correct. Then inspect the sparking plug; unscrew it from the cylinder and lay it on the top fins with the high tension cable connected to it in the usual way, but do not let the cable terminal touch the cylinder. Then rotate the engine with the kick-starter, or by turning round the fly-wheel. If no sparking is noticeable between the sparking plug points it will show that the plug is the cause of your difficulty. It should be dismantled and carefully cleaned, all soot being removed from its insulation, because this is probably causing the current to short circuit instead of jumping the points, and creating a spark. Reassemble the sparking plug and carefully adjust the points, so that a distance of not more than $\frac{1}{32}$ in. separates them. Presuming that when tested there is a satisfactory spark at the plug points, and the engine still refuses to fire, examine the high-tension cable from the magneto to the sparking plug. This may have been touching the cylinder, with the result that the rubber covering has burned, and the inner wire is touching a metal part of the machine, thus causing a short circuit. The only satisfactory remedy then is to fit a new cable. Another point at which trouble may occur, but this is very unusual, is at the "pick-up" spring inside the magneto. At the magneto end of the high tension cable is a vulcanite terminal held in position by a spring clip. This terminal should be taken out, and it will be seen to contain a small spring which makes contact with the ignition coil (see Fig. 55). This spring should be quite straight, so that when the terminal is in position it touches the small contact point on the coil, immediately underneath it. Should the spring show signs of having been bent sideways it has probably not made proper contact, and your trouble lies there.

A Final Word about Sparking Plugs. The manufacturers, who carry out extensive and prolonged tests, really do know the type of sparking plug best suited for each particular engine, and, therefore, if occasion arises to fit a new sparking plug, it should always be of the correct type as that shown in the chart below. It is often a costly matter to experiment with different sparking plugs, because an unsuitable one can quite easily do considerable damage, although this is not appreciated by many riders.

SPARKING PLUG CHART

	1	2	*LODGE 3	4	K.L.G.	CHAMPION	WIPAC (non-detachable)	PACY (detachable)
98 c.c. Midget	BBL	C3	H1	H1P	M.50	8 Com	P.8	18S
98 c.c. Junior	CN	C14	HN	NNP	F.50	L-10	P.4S	14H.T
98 c.c. Junior de luxe	BBL	CB3	HLS	HLIP	ML.30	7 Com-L	P.8	18L
98 c.c. Mk. 1 F	C14	H14	HH14	HNP	F.70	L-10S	P.4	14S
98 c.c. Mk. 2 F	C14	H14	HH14	HNP	F.70	L-10S	P.4	14S
98 c.c. Mk. 3 F	C14	H14	HH14	HNP	F.70	L-10S	P.4	14S
98 c.c. Mk. 4 F	C14	H14	HH14	HNP	F.70	L-10S	P.4	14S
125 c.c. Mk. VIII D	C3	H1	H1	H1P	M.60	16	—	18T
125 c.c. Mk. IX D	C3	H1	H1	H1P	M.60	16	—	18T
122 c.c. Mk. 10 D	C14	H14	HH14	HNP	F.70	L-10S	P.4	14S
147 c.c. VIII C.	BBL	C3	H1	H1P	M.30	L-10S	P.4	14T
147 c.c. 24 C	C3	H3	H3	H1P	M.80	8 Com	P.4T	18S
147 c.c. 25 C	BBL	C3	H1	H1P	M.30	7 Com-L	P.8	18S
147 c.c. 26 C	C3	H3	H3	H1P	M.80	8 Com	P.8	18S
148 c.c. Mk. XII C	BBL	CB3	HLS	HL1P	ML.30	8 Com-L	P.8	18L
148 c.c. Mk. X C	C3	H3	H3	H1P	M.30	8 Com	P.8	18S
148 c.c. Mk. XI C	C3	H3	H3	H1P	M.30	8 Com	P.8	18S
148 c.c. Mk. 31 C	HN	HH14	3HN	HNP	F.70	L-11S	P.4T	14T
172 c.c. Sports	BBL	CB3	HLS	HL1P	ML.30	7 Com-L	P.8	18L
172 c.c. Super Sports	CB3	HLS	HLS	HL1P	ML.30	16	P.8	18L
173 c.c. Mk. 2 L	HN	HH14	3HN	HNP	F.70	L-11S	P.4T	14T
196 c.c. Super Sports	CB3	HLS	HLS	HLTP	ML.60	7 Com-L	P.8	18L
196 c.c. Mk. 1 E	BBL	CB3	HLS	HL1P	ML.30	7 Com-L	P.8	18L
196 c.c. Mk. 2 E	BBL	CB3	HLS	HL1P	ML.30	7 Com-L	P.8	18L
196 c.c. Mk. 3 E	BBL	CB3	HLS	HL1P	ML.30	7 Com-L	P.8	18L
196 c.c. Mk. 5 E	CB3	HLS	HLS	HL1P	ML.60	16	P.8	18L
197 c.c. Mk. 6 E	HN	HH14	3HN	HNP	F.70	L-11S	P.4T	14T
197 c.c. Mk. 8 E	HN	HH14	3HN	HNP	F.70	L-11S	P.4T	14T
197 c.c. Mk. 9 E	HN	HH14	3HN	HNP	F.70	L-11S	P.4T	14T
249 c.c. Mk. XIV A	CB3	CB3	HLS	HL1P	ML.30	7 Com-L	P.8	18L
249 c.c. Mk. XIV	CB3	CB3	HLS	HL1P	ML.30	7 Com-L	P.8	18L
324 c.c. Mk. 2 T	—	HH14	—	—	—	—	—	—
249 c.c. Mk. 3 T	—	HH14	—	—	—	—	—	—
346 c.c. Mk. XIV B	CB3	CB3	HLS	HL1P	ML.30	7 Com-L	P.8	18L
346 c.c. Mk. 17 A.	CB3	CB3	HLS	HL1P	ML.30	7 Com-L	P.8	18L
346 c.c. Mk. 18 A	CB3	CB3	HLS	HL1P	ML.30	7 Com-L	P.8	18L
346 c.c. Mk. XI A	CB3	CB3	HLS	HL1P	ML.30	7 Com-L	P.8	18L
346 c.c. Mk. XI B	CB3	CB3	HLS	HL1P	ML.30	7 Com-L	P.8	18L
346 c.c. Mk. XV A	CB3	CB3	HLS	HL1P	ML.30	7 Com-L	P.8	18L
346 c.c. Mk. XV 3	CB3	CB3	HLS	HL1P	ML.30	7 Com-L	P.8	18L

FORWARD: 14 mm. Standard reach . D.14   18 mm. Standard reach . D.18

*1. For when engine is oiling plugs   2. For normal running   3. For hard driving or if plug is overheating   4. Platinum pointed plugs

Fly-wheel Magneto Types. 2-*Pole*. This original and successful model, for ignition only, was later fitted with a.c. lighting coils. 3-*Pole*. This gives both ignition and lighting and has proved eminently successful for the Junior-de-luxe autocycle. 4-*Pole*. The plate carried an ignition coil and two lighting coils. 6-*Pole*. Both ignition and lighting coils are fitted, the latter having separate coils for head and rear lamps giving an output of either 18 or 24 watts at 6 volts. *Improved* 6-*Pole*. This has an armature plate assembly of unique and new design which gives a much greater lighting output.

The information in this chapter, however, refers in general to all of them, and the different patterns do not require detailed description.

CHAPTER VII
THE VILLIERS CARBURETTOR

THE object of the carburettor is to supply the engine with a mixture of petrol and air combined in such proportions as to make an explosive compound. Varying engine temperature and load conditions make the problem of carburation rather complex, and even the most modern instrument is really a compromise, but, nevertheless, an efficient one.

Petrol is a spirit distilled from crude oil, and having a specific gravity of $0 \cdot 76$, for the interest of those readers who are technically inclined. It is essential for this spirit to vaporize rapidly, and an efficient carburettor will help to do this. Some fuels are less easily vaporized than others, and that is why it is advisable always to use No. 1 quality of one of the well-known brands of petrol, rather than to employ an inferior fuel in an endeavour to save a copper or two per gallon.

Briefly, the action of a carburettor is as follows.

Liquid petrol issues through a minute nozzle into a stream of rapidly moving air, by which process it is converted from liquid fuel into a highly atomized vapour. The upward stroke of the piston sucks this air stream through the carburettor, and the amount that is allowed to pass into the engine is controlled by the throttle slide. It is obvious that the strength of the mixture depends upon the proportion of fuel emerging from the jet, and the air passing through the carburettor.

In most instruments the size of jet is fixed, so that a set quantity of petrol with air, giving a certain proportion, is constantly fed to the engine. This proportion is determined for average running, but obviously it must be required to vary this according to different engine conditions, because at times a much richer mixture, i.e. a greater proportion of petrol in the air, may be needed.

In the Villiers instrument, the amount of petrol that is allowed to issue from the jet is automatically proportioned to the amount of air that is allowed to enter into the engine, from which it will be seen that this instrument must be more efficient, covering a wider range of varying engine conditions than would a carburettor with a fixed jet or nozzle.

A detailed description of the working of the Villiers carburettor is given as follows.

Construction. The Villiers carburettor gives a perfectly and automatically adjusted mixture over the whole range of throttle opening. This is achieved by means of its compensating action, which is very simple and involves the use of absolutely no moving parts.

Being entirely automatic in its operation, the instrument requires only one lever to control it. Such an arrangement is

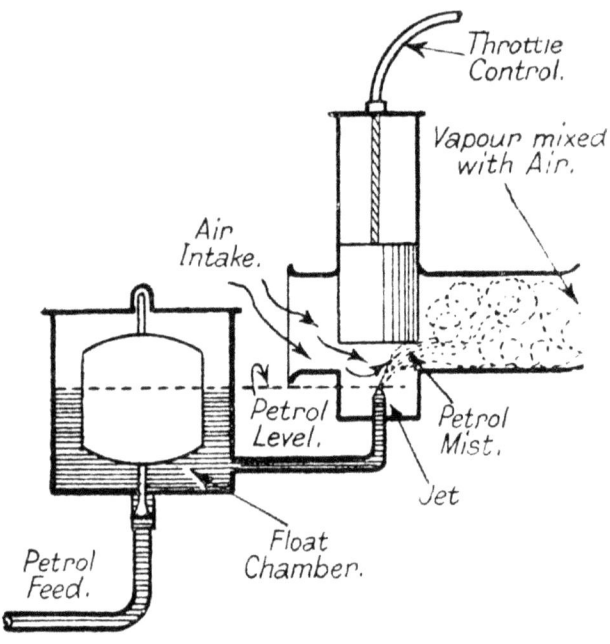

Fig. 57. Diagram Explaining the Principle of Carburation

better than having one air and one throttle slide, each controlled with a separate lever, because with the latter arrangement the rider is always over-correcting his mixture. He finds the setting is a little too weak, and therefore closes his air lever. The effect of altering the air setting on an engine is not instantaneous, and, therefore, by the time the engine has settled down to the new air setting, it is found that the mixture is too rich and the lever has again to be opened a little. This goes on repeatedly, and the rider rarely has a proper mixture setting.

All this is obviated in the Villiers instrument, because there is only one lever to open and close the throttle, which, at the same time, enlarges or reduces the size of the jet by means of a taper needle attached to and working with the throttle.

An independent adjustment of this taper needle is provided to

THE VILLIERS CARBURETTOR

give a specially rich mixture at times when it is required, such as when starting a cold engine. This independent adjustment is provided on some models by means of a rod (*d* in Fig. 58A) having a quick-thread in the throttle, which is arranged to raise or lower the needle ¼ in. by one complete turn of the bar. On other models the needle is raised and lowered in the jet by means of a separate control (*d* in Fig. 58B) operated from the handlebar.

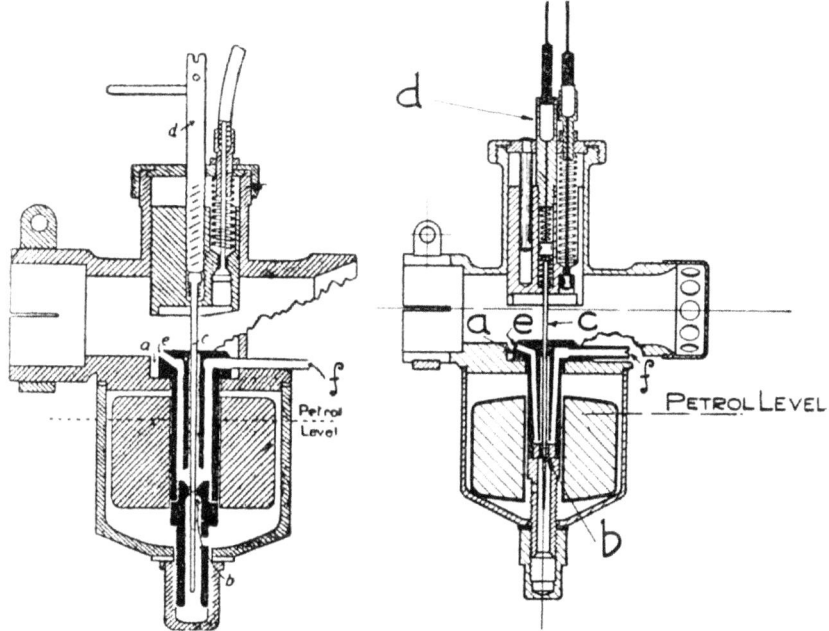

Fig. 58A. The Single Lever Carburettor

Fig. 58B. The Double Lever Carburettor

The handlebar lever is marked " rich " and " weak " to indicate how the jet size is set. *On no account must this top lever be used as an ordinary " air control." It should remain stationary except when deliberately wishing to alter the size of the jet.*

The lightweight carburettor fits on a one-inch stub and the middleweight on a 1⅛-in. stub and the latter has larger ports. Both single- and double-lever types are made and are shown in Figs. 58A and 58B.

The action of the carburettor is very simple, and reference to Figs. 58A and 58B, showing sectional arrangements of these two types of carburettor, will make the action clear. Depressing the float tickler creates a well of petrol at *a*, which, with the throttle open only a little, is drawn into the cylinder at the first kick, so giving very easy starting. The opening and closing of the throttle, as already explained, enlarges and reduces the size of the jet b by means of the taper needle c. The size of the jet may be enlarged independently of the throttle opening, to give a rich mixture when starting from cold, the " rich " and " weak " positions being marked on the top disk of the carburettor, or on the handle-bar lever top plate. When the engine is warmed up the needle is again lowered in the jet, to weaken the mixture as much as is consistent with good running. The position of the needle will then not require to be altered again until the engine is started from cold.

The automatic compensating action of the carburettor is as follows. Mixture is delivered by the carburettor in two different ways—firstly, by the suction of the engine on the orifice e, and secondly, by the force of the head of petrol through jet b. Since the jet b is below petrol level, petrol is always issuing from it.

The suction of the engine on the orifice e draws in a stream of air through the compensating tube f across the top of the jet b, where it mixes with and breaks up the petrol, and so issues from e into the main air stream as a partially atomized vapour.

If the load on the engine is increased, so reducing the engine speed, as for instance, when hill climbing, the suction on the orifice e is reduced. This would weaken the mixture but for the fact that the petrol issuing from jet b is constant, thereby richening the partially atomized vapour coming through e—the combined effect being that the mixture strength is maintained constant irrespective of engine speed or load.

As the main jet is in the centre of the float chamber the mixture is not upset by tilting the machine, and actually the motor-cycle must almost lie down before flooding will occur.

The Villiers carburettor has been improved by interposing a toggle arrangement between the float and fuel needle and is now fitted on all models. It is similar to the fitment on the heavy-weight carburettor shown on page 91.

Important. If the carburettor fitted to your machine is the Villiers model with two control levers on the handlebar, it cannot be too definitely emphasized that the top lever is not an air control as on other instruments, and must not be used as such. It is solely a lever for independently altering the size of the jet to give an extra rich mixture when required, such as when starting a cold engine.

On the single-lever Villiers carburettor, this control takes the form of a small bar on the top of the carburettor itself. Both should be turned toward " rich " only when starting from cold, and then should be kept as far towards the " weak " position as is consistent with good running.

THE VILLIERS CARBURETTOR

Tuning for Best All-round Results. Being self-regulating, and provided the correct jet and needle are fitted, the carburettor will give the right mixture at all throttle openings and speeds, and the independent jet control should not need to be moved when the engine is warm until again starting from cold. This carburettor is adaptable to any type of engine, but various models require a different combination of jet and needle. Early Villiers carburettors had only one compensating tube (f in Fig. 58A), but later models are fitted with two. The following are the standard jets and needles used with each Villiers engine—

STANDARD CARBURETTOR SETTINGS

Capacity c.c.	Type of Engine	Type of Carburettor	Jet No.	Needle Taper
98	Midget	Midget	8	$5\frac{1}{2}$ midget
98	Junior	Junior	8.J	2
98	Junior-de-luxe	Junior	7J	2
98	1 F	6/0	8 (6/0)	20 (6/0)
98	2 F	Junior	8 J	$2\frac{1}{2}$
122	9 D, VIII D	Midget	8	6
122	9 D	L/W	3	3
122	9 D	L/W 3/1	3	3 special
122	10 D	3/4	0·083	3
147	VI C, VII C, VIII C	L/W	3	$2\frac{1}{2}$
147	30 C	S.19	80	$3\frac{1}{2}$
147	29 C	S.25	130	$3\frac{1}{2}$
148	XII C, XV C	M/W	2	4
148	31 C range	S.19	$2\frac{1}{2}$	$3\frac{1}{2}$
172	Sports	M/W	3	3
172	T.T. Super sports	M/W	3	$3\frac{1}{2}$
173	2 L range	S.22	$2\frac{1}{2}$	$3\frac{1}{2}$
196	1 E	M/W	3	$3\frac{1}{2}$
196	2 E	M/W	2	4
196	3 E	M/W	2	5
196	Super Sports	M/W	2	4
196	7 E, 8 E	S.25	120	$3\frac{1}{2}$
197	6 E	4/5	0·081	$4\frac{1}{2}$
197	9 E range	S.25	3	$3\frac{1}{2}$
225	1 H	S.25	120	$3\frac{1}{2}$
247	VI A, VII A	M/W	3	$2\frac{1}{2}$
247	VIII A	M/W	3	3
247	IX A	M/W	3	4
247	X A, XVI A	M/W	2	5
249	XIV A (air-cooled)	M/W	2	5
249	XIV A (water-cooled)	M/W	2	6
249	XVII A, XVIII A	M/W	51	2 special
249	2 T	S.22/2	Pilot 35	$3\frac{1}{2}$
324	3 T	S.22/2	Main 170, 180 or 190	$3\frac{1}{2}$
346	XIV B	M/W	2	5
353	28 B	S.24	120	$3\frac{1}{2}$

All needles are marked with the degree of taper on their side.

The following sizes of needles are available: 1½, 2, 2½, 3, 3½, 4, 4½, 5, 6, and 7, but those given in the table above are the ones found most suitable for general running. Size 0·081 jets are marked with that figure on their head, but the other jets are marked with a figure on one of the flats of the hexagon, half way down the shank.

If it is necessary to write to the makers for any spare parts for a carburettor, always give particulars of your engine.

To tune the carburettor, first obtain the most satisfactory position of the needle for slow running on the road when the engine is warm, by altering the jet control lever, and then open the throttle lever quickly. If the engine dies out it shows that the mixture is too weak, and therefore a needle with a greater degree of taper should be fitted. If it is found possible to open it quickly and the engine is inclined to " hunt," the mixture is obviously too rich, and a needle with less taper should be fitted. Again, the mixture is shown to be too rich if the throttle is closed when running at speed and the engine hesitates, or momentarily ceases to fire. When the needle best suited for speed is obtained it will be the best one for economy and power. There is no definite rule as to the best running position of the jet lever, but it is wise to set it so that when turned as far as it will go to the weak position, the mixture is actually too weak to run. This means that for normal running it will have to be a little way towards rich, and will always give a margin of safety. Otherwise, if it were as far as it would go in the weak position, one would never be quite certain that one was running on the best setting. If necessary, in the case of the single-lever carburettor, the small bar should be unscrewed from the needle rod, and replaced in another hole at right angles to the previous one, so that the needle rod may be turned round farther.

In the case of the two-lever carburettor there is a screw with a locknut on the body of the handlebar control. By screwing this in the mixture is made weaker, and by screwing it out it is made richer. It is very necessary that at all times the compensating tubes are clear. Should one be lost, on no account must this be replaced by a screw or plug.

To Change the Needle—Single-lever Model. Unscrew the top cap on the body of the carburettor and remove the throttle. Unscrew the bar on the needle rod, and then the needle rod itself. Now by inverting the throttle, the needle with its small spring will fall out (see Fig. 59). Fit this small spring, or preferably a new one, to the new needle you wish to install, making sure that the small coil of the spring is at the top of the needle. Place the needle in the throttle, screw in the needle rod, and then replace the throttle in the body of the carburettor, making sure

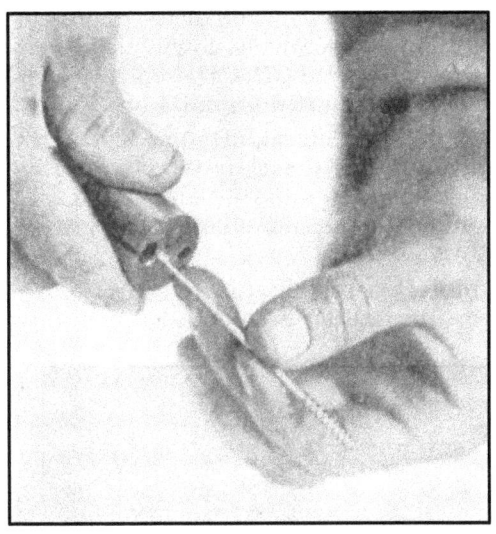

Fig. 59. Refitting the Taper Needle in the Villiers Carburettor (Early Type)

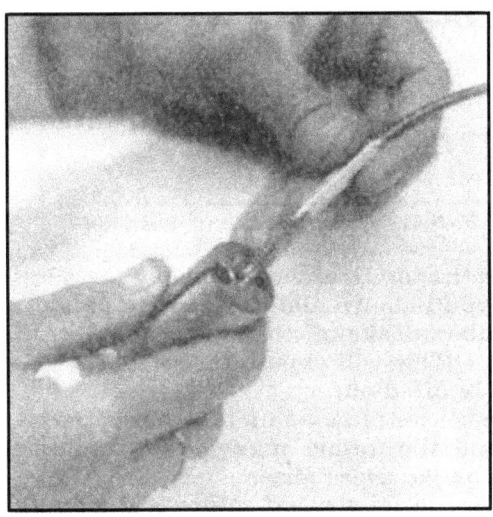

Fig. 60. Showing How to Remove the Taper Needle from the Throttle of the Two-lever Carburettor

that the top disk is located by means of its tongue in the slot on the carburettor body before screwing down the top ring. Tighten the small bar in the needle rod after the correct adjustment has been obtained, so that this part does not work loose.

Two-lever Model. This differs slightly in construction, and after the throttle is taken out of the carburettor the hexagon in which the cable takes its anchorage must be unscrewed. This will give access to the needle, which is then changed as on the single-lever model (see Fig. 60).

Dismantling and Reassembling the Carburettor. The instrument should not be dismantled before first detaching it from the

FIG. 61. FUEL NEEDLE IN POSITION
(EARLIER TYPE)

engine. Unscrew the top ring and remove the throttle, then turn the carburettor upside down and unscrew the nut at the bottom of the float chamber. Take off the fibre washer, then lift off the cup and the float. This will expose the small fuel needle, which should be carefully lifted out.

To remove the centre piece and jet, unscrew the compensating tube or tubes, and the former may then be pulled out. *Never unscrew the jet from the centre piece.*

Filter gauzes are usually fitted inside the nipple connexions and must be carefully cleaned and replaced.

When reassembling, clean each part carefully. First place the centre piece in position with the fibre washer under its head, then screw in the compensating tube, or tubes, carefully. Place the fuel needle in position, making sure that the *pointed end is inside* the carburettor body. Place the float on top of this, and then

Fig. 62. When Dismantling the Villiers Carburettor, be Careful that the Fuel Needle is not Lost

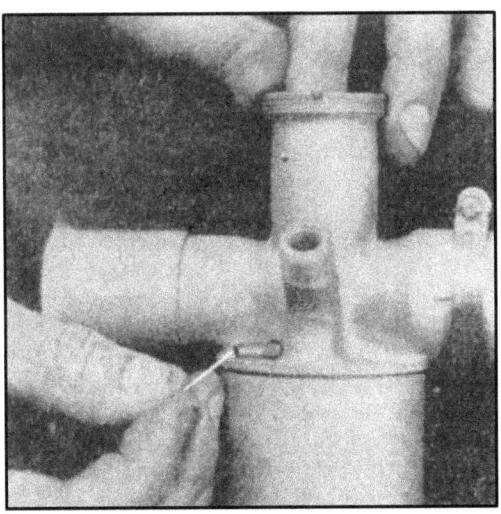

Fig. 63. The Compensating Tubes in the Villiers Carburettor Must be Free from Obstruction

after fitting the large fibre washer, put on the cup, then the small fibre washer, and screw the bottom nut into position. Tighten the latter with a spanner, but do not use too much force.

For some years now an improvement has been incorporated in the form of a damper spring fitted inside the throttle. This achieves the same object as the bulging of the rod to prevent jarring round of the needle rod, and has the advantage of being quite permanent and needing no further attention.

The Needle Rod in the Old Pattern Single-lever Instrument. If this rod loses its tension, and tends to turn round on its own accord, it should be taken out, and the slotted end of the thread may be opened slightly so as to give the rod more tension. The best way of doing this is to place a small bar about $\frac{1}{16}$ in. in diameter in the slots, approximately $\frac{1}{8}$ in. from the end, and then close the ends of the rod together with a pair of pliers (see Fig. 64).

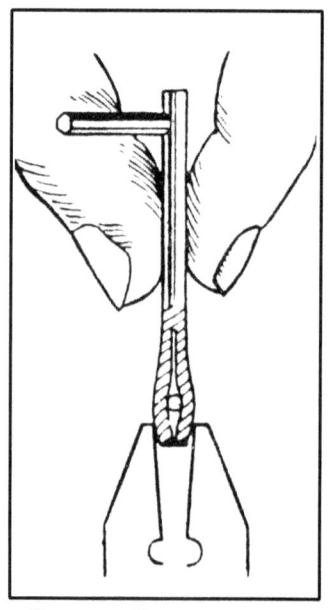

FIG. 64. TIGHTENING THE NEEDLE ROD

The Needle Rod in the Modern Single-lever Lightweight and Middleweight Models. These have an improvement in the needle rod, known as the "damper spring." The needle rod is held in position by a damper spring which prevents it moving except when turned by hand.

The needle rod is split at the quick-thread end, and into the split is inserted a special shaped spring, which in plan view looks like the letter S.

The top and bottom of the S press against the sides of a hole in the throttle slide, and thus by friction prevent the needle rod turning on its own accord, due to vibration.

When detaching the petrol pipe from the tank to the carburettor, this should be handled carefully, and the union nuts should never be wrenched.

Be sure the spanner is a good fit on the nuts, and, when undoing the top union, it is advisable to get another spanner to hold the hexagon on the tap, so that this does not unscrew with the pipe union.

When replacing the petrol pipe, tighten the top and bottom unions together. This is much easier than screwing one up

THE VILLIERS CARBURETTOR

perfectly tight and then endeavouring to get the other nipple into position.

The Air Cleaner. Such a fitment as this is always worth while on every machine, and is usually fitted by the maker.

The air cleaner is fitted on to the air intake side of the carburettor, and prevents dirt and grit passing into the engine. The old pre-war model has a number of vanes on its outer face which give a spinning motion to the air, and a deflector inside flings it outwards, where it is trapped by a lip in the shell of the cleaner. Any particles of dust are ejected here, and the cleaned air passes without obstruction into the carburettor. There are no moving parts to get out of order, and no gauze which may clog. Consequently, this cleaner requires no attention.

This air cleaner has been superseded by an oil-wetted type, and with a suitable screwed adaptor can easily be fitted to most of the motor-cycle and industrial types of Villiers engines. This should be cleaned every 1,500 miles by swilling the filter in petrol, drying and swabbing with engine oil, draining, and then refitting.

The "1100" Air Cleaner. Carburettors Type S.19, S.22, and S.25 can be fitted with a newly designed air cleaner with the large filtering area of 55 sq. in. It is standard to the Mark 9 E Trials and Sports Units but should certainly be used on all models to prevent undue wear from dust.

The Villiers Midget Carburettor. This small carburettor is the result of very extensive tests carried out to find a simple and efficient carburettor. It has a minimum of adjustments. The design of the carburettor is similar in principle to the present Villiers larger models, yet modified in details to enable the absolute novice to get good results.

It gives perfectly correct mixture over the whole range of throttle opening, and this is achieved by its compensating action which is similar to the larger models. It is very simple and involves the use of no moving parts. Being entirely automatic, it only requires one lever to control it, and is much better than having one air and one throttle slide, each controlled by a separate lever. It eliminates trouble in correcting the mixture, which is essential in the majority of makes of carburettors. With the Villiers "Midget" carburettor (Fig. 65) there is only one lever, which opens and closes the throttle, and at the same time enlarges or reduces the size of the jet E by means of a tapered needle C, attached to and working with the throttle G. An independent adjustment of this tapered needle C is provided by taking out the throttle G and loosening the screw K. This will enable the needle C to be adjusted, for a richer or weaker mixture, whichever is required. This adjustment of the needle C is for the purpose of the initial setting to suit individual engines, and to allow for slight variations of engine running. The action of the carburettor is very simple, and the reference to Fig. 65, showing the sectional arrangement of the carburettor, will make it clear.

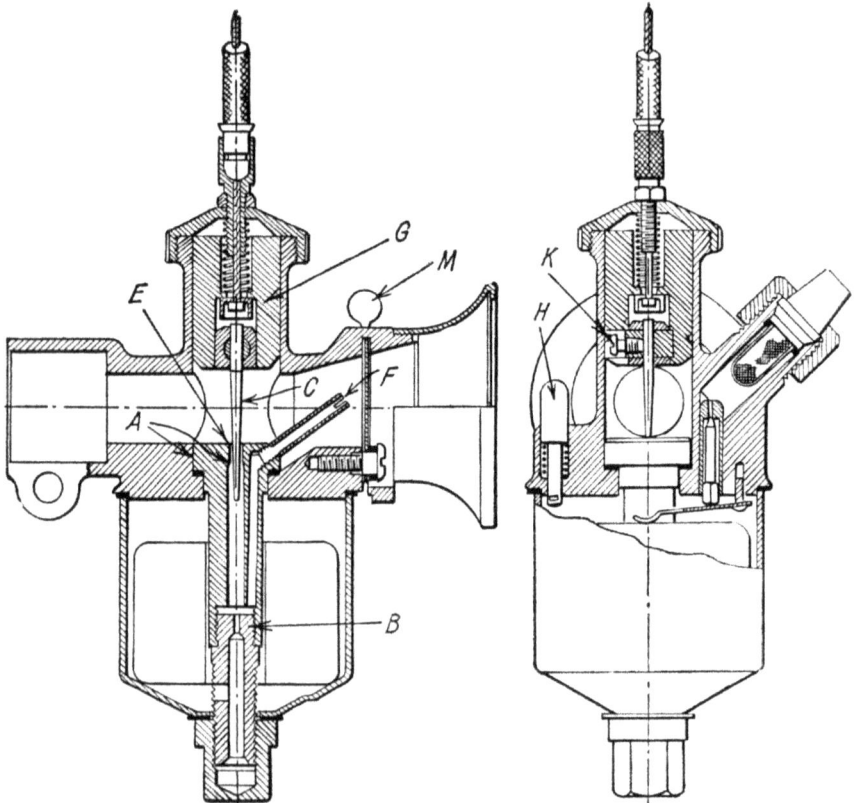

FIG. 65. THE "MIDGET" CARBURETTOR

Depressing the float tickler H creates a well of petrol at A, which with the throttle open only a little is drawn in the cylinder at the first kick, so giving very easy starting.

The opening and closing of the throttle, as already explained, enlarges and reduces the size of the jet E by means of the tapered needle C.

An easy start is obtained from cold by turning the strangler plate M at the inlet end of the carburettor, until it covers the hole. This should be left in this position until the engine is slightly warm (or, a good sign, if the engine begins to four-stroke) when the plate should be lowered.

When on the road the automatic compensating action of the

carburettor adjusts the strength of the mixture to the demands of load or speed as follows—

As the engine speed increases, the suction on the orifice E also increases, but owing to the fact that air offers less resistance than petrol, air is drawn through the compensating tube F across the jet B, mixing with the petrol issuing from this jet, and so gradually weakening the mixture. As the engine speed falls, such as when hill climbing, the suction on the orifice E also falls and, therefore, less air is drawn down the tube F. As the jet B, however, is below the petrol level, a constant mixture is maintained.

It will be seen from the above, that at no time does neat petrol pass into the engine from the orifice E, but only a mixed vapour of petrol and air, varying in strength according to the demand of the engine, and controlled automatically by the amount of air passing across the top of the jet B. As the main jet is in the centre of the float chamber, the mixture is not upset by tilting the machine, and actually the motor-cycle must almost lie down before flooding will occur. The automatic compensating action, which is the principal feature of the Villiers carburettor, gives remarkable flexibility and great economy, because the engine is working more efficiently, as it has the correct mixture strength at all times.

The midget carburettor, in common with the modern Lightweight and Middleweight types, has a toggle control to the fuel needle which gives an increase in leverage over the old design and consequently overcomes any tendency to flood.

If it becomes necessary to remove the fuel needle, proceed as follows: unscrew the top ring and remove the throttle, then the compensating tube from centre piece. The compensating tube has a slotted end which is exposed after removal of the air filter. Remove the bottom nut which secures the float. The centre piece can then be pushed upwards until the toggle can swing to one side, when the fuel needle will drop.

The Villiers Junior and Mark 2 F Unit Carburettor. This carburettor is fitted on the Junior Engine, and the principle is exactly the same as the Midget type carburettor, but a different method is used for the adjustment of the needle. To adjust the needle, firstly remove the throttle by unscrewing the top ring. At the head of the throttle there is a small slotted screw; turning this in a clockwise direction, which lowers the needle, will give a weaker setting. Turning in an anti-clockwise direction will give a richer setting. For adjustment, give approximately half a turn at a time until found to be correct.

To dismantle the carburettor, proceed as for the Midget type, except that the centre piece is located by a small screw at the bottom and outside of the throttle chamber.

The Villiers Heavyweight Type Carburettor was made for the Mark XVIII A engine and used for the early Mark 3 E engines.

To Start Engine from Cold. Press tickler (T) Fig 66 (b), until flooding occurs, open jet control lever to full rich position, and open throttle about one-third. One or two kicks on the starter should start the engine. When warm close jet lever as required until in set position at bottom of slide.

Pilot Jet. This jet (a) governs the carburettor up to approximately one-quarter throttle; to enrich, screw clockwise.

Needle (N). No. 2 is fitted as standard to suit conditions in England. If the acceleration is poor, raise needle; if acceleration is still poor fit No. 3 needle. If the engine four-strokes at one-third throttle opening, the mixture is too rich. Fit No. 1 needle.

Main Jet (J). This jet (a) governs "all out" speed, and has no effect on small throttle openings.

To adjust the needle unscrew the top sleeve (S) out of the slide, and withdraw needle control complete Extract the small "U" shaped wire (W) and re-insert in another groove in the needle, raising the latter to get a richer setting, and lowering it to get a weaker one.

Needles are marked one, two, etc., on the extreme top.

Petrol filter (F) should be cleaned periodically or petrol will not flow freely. On no account should it be taken off the union, or grit, etc., will get into the needle seating (C) and cause flooding. Keep the air filter gauze (G) clear of dirt, etc., by washing in petrol. Spares are still obtainable for the limited number still in use.

A Few Carburettor Troubles and their Causes—Constant Flooding. This may be due to a punctured float which allows the petrol to find its way inside, and therefore makes it too heavy, and so causes the float chamber to fill and overflow. Or, to dirt on the seating of the fuel needle, preventing it from closing properly.

If the float is punctured, it is as well to replace it, because repairing it with solder may make it too heavy.

Another reason for flooding may be the " tickler " jamming down, caused by grit being thrown on to it from the road. To free it, tap gently and pull the tickler up. Clean carefully.

Spitting Back. This is the symptom of too weak a mixture, and may be caused by—

(*a*) Incorrect setting of the control levers, in which case the jet control must be set further towards " rich."

(*b*) Dirty gauze or filter.

(*c*) The fuel needle stuck in its seating, preventing **petrol** flowing to the carburettor.

THE VILLIERS CARBURETTOR

(d) A choked petrol pipe.
(e) Water in the petrol.
(f) The vent hole in the petrol tank or carburettor body choked.

N.B. It is impossible for a choked jet to occur on the Villiers carburettor, owing to the needle which constantly works inside the jet.

There is usually a small hole in the filler tank to allow air to pass into the petrol tank to compensate for the petrol drawn out.

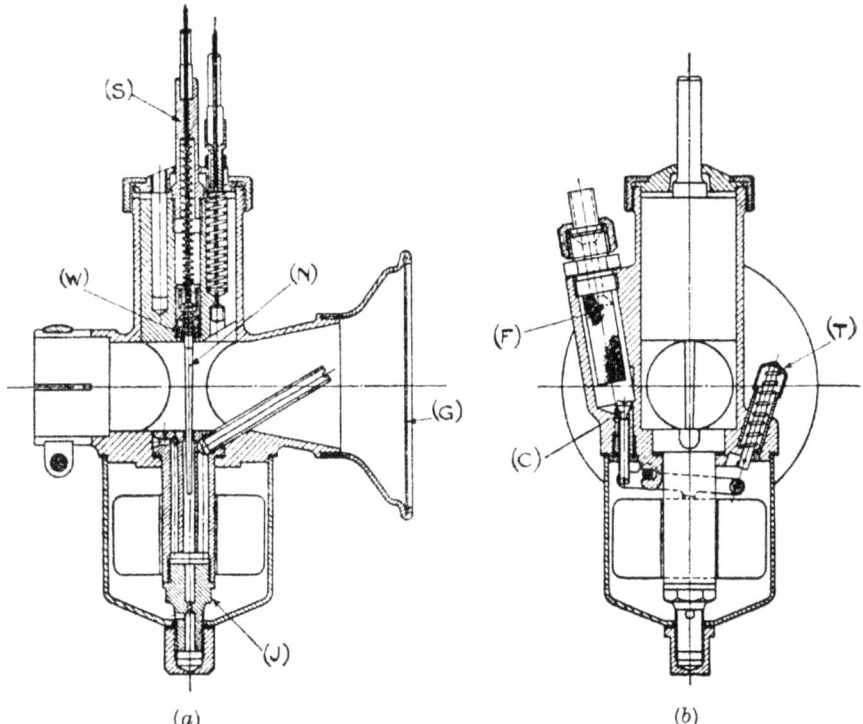

Fig. 66. The Villiers Heavyweight Carburettor

If this is choked, a partial vacuum will be created in the tank and obstruct the flow of petrol.

Carburettor will Not Shut Off. This may be due to the throttle sticking, probably through mud or grit causing it to bind. This would be prevented if an air cleaner were fitted. Another cause may be a damaged control cable, preventing the inner wire from moving freely in the outer cable; or to incorrect adjustment of the cable screw.

CHAPTER VIII

THE VILLIERS ELECTRIC LIGHTING SYSTEMS

NOWADAYS, electric lighting is universal on motor-cycles, and this is due very largely to the introduction of the Villiers fly-wheel magneto, which produces electric current for lighting purposes. Motor-cycles fitted with all types of Villiers engines since the early Mark IV models have fly-wheel magnetos, and can, therefore, be fully equipped with electric lighting, which has, of course, so many advantages.

There are four distinct systems of Villiers lighting: i.e. the direct lighting, the accumulator charging set, the dynamo charging set, and the parking light set. In the former, as its name implies, the current goes to the lamps direct, and, consequently, a light is always obtainable when the engine is running, but when it stops it ceases to generate current. In the accumulator charging set, which is now obsolete, the current is converted by means of a commutator and charges an accumulator from which the light is obtained, even when the engine is not running. Dynamo charging and parking light sets are not now made but many are still in operation and the hints given in this chapter will no doubt prove of value.

Descriptions of Villiers lighting sets are given in the following pages.

The Direct Lighting Set. The wiring in this system is exceedingly simple, and so far as the rider is concerned consists only of one cable taken from a plug in the back of the armature plate of the fly-wheel magneto to the head lamp, and thence to the tail lamp, the two being wired " in series," which is an electrical term denoting that the current passes through one lamp before it goes to the next (see Fig. 67). On all these lighting sets the light is controlled by an " on " and " off " switch situated at the back of the head lamp. From time to time improvements have been made in the lamps, and it has also been possible to increase the output of current from the coils which has necessitated using stronger bulbs. The table on page 92 will show at a glance the bulbs that should be fitted in order to make the best use of your lighting set.

Owing to its simplicity there is very little likelihood of the rider being stranded on the road with this lighting set. Should the filament of one bulb break, perhaps through vibration, the other

ELECTRIC LIGHTING SYSTEMS

Type of Engine	Head Lamp	Tail Lamp
Early pattern engines fitted with large fly-wheel magneto (fly-wheel diameter, $8\frac{1}{4}$ in.)	4 volt 0·35 amp.	4 volt 0·5 amp.
Engines with small fly-wheel magneto (fly-wheel diameter, 7 in.)	6 volt 0·75 amp.	4 volt 0·75 amp.

bulb will go out owing to the set being wired in series. To get home, a temporary repair can be made by fitting the tail lamp bulb into the head lamp if the bulb in the latter has broken, and then breaking the glass of the damaged bulb, fitting it into the tail

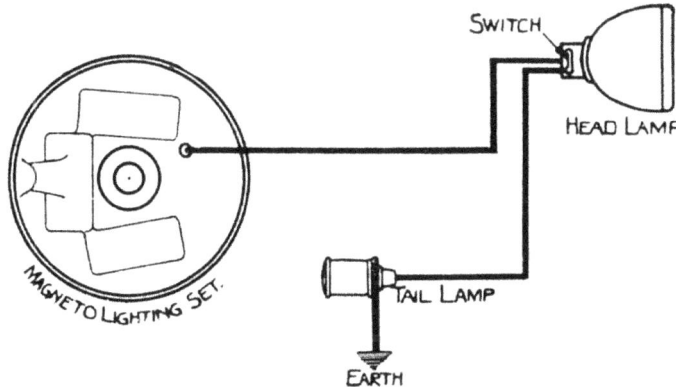

Fig. 67. Wiring Diagram of Direct Lighting System

lamp and twisting the two ends of the broken filament together. This will complete the circuit and enable a light at the head lamp to be obtained.

The connexion on the magneto end consists of a split terminal at the end of the cable, which is pushed into its socket. This terminal must be kept quite clean to give good contact, and if it shows a tendency to become loose and vibrate from its holder, the two prongs of the terminal should be opened out slightly to give them a greater pressure against the sides of the socket. On one early type of Villiers lighting set a dry battery was incorporated (see Fig. 73). The system of lighting the head lamp direct from the magneto was maintained, but the dry battery was added as a stand-by to give a light when the machine was standing, and a two-way switch was provided for this purpose. The battery employed was of the dry cell type, and needed replacing completely when run down after approximately 36 hours' continuous use.

Lamps. The following short description and diagrams explain exactly how to dismantle (should access to the bulbs be required, or the lamps need focusing) the various types of lamps used from time to time in Villiers lighting sets. This information will also serve for the lamps (Fig. 76) employed in the accumulator charging set, described later.

The earliest pattern lamp is shown diagrammatically in Fig. 68. This is dismantled by removing the plug adaptor A and lock nut B from the holder. Then unscrew the wing nut C and push the screwed portion forward. With this inner shell released from the outer casing F, remove the split ring G and the glass case H, when the bulb J can then be taken out and the bulb holder unscrewed from the inner shell.

The second type of small head lamp employed is shown in Fig. 69. The front D should be pressed forward and twisted in a clockwise direction, when it may be pulled away from the body of the lamp and the bulb exposed. To adjust the focus in this head lamp, unscrew the lock nut C, and turn bulb holder E in the required direction until a satisfactory focus has been obtained, and then lock it into position with the nut C.

The head lamp used with the old pattern lighting set incorporating the dry battery is shown in Fig. 70. To remove the bulb unscrew the bolt B, thus opening the wedge lock ring A which draws the front of the lamp tight against the body. Turn the front of the lamp C in an anti-clockwise direction to release it, and when replacing see that the front of the lamp engages in the slots before twisting it to the right and tightening up the wedge lock ring at the back. Another type of lamp used on old pattern direct lighting sets is shown in Fig. 71. This is distinguished by being larger than the previous models, and by the large screwdriver slot at the back of the lamp. The switch in this instance is underneath the lamp and not at the back, as on the previous lamps described. In this the screws at A must be slackened to enable the front B to be pulled off to give access to the bulb. This lamp is focused by turning the screw C in the back of the lamp in the required direction, which moves the bulb holder backwards and forwards along its slot.

A later type of head lamp was available in two sizes, one $4\frac{1}{2}$-in. diameter and the other 6-in. diameter. On these the front must be pressed in and twisted in an anti-clockwise direction to remove it. The bulb may then be taken out, and if it is required to focus the lamp, draw off the reflector and slacken the thumbscrew. The bulb holder can then be pushed backwards and forwards in

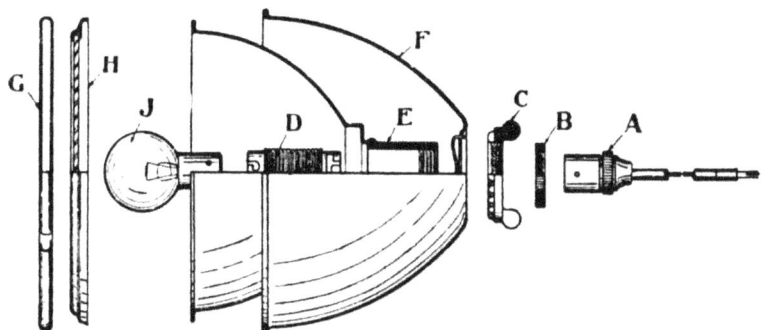

Fig. 68. Means for Focusing and Adjusting the Villiers Head Lamp, Early Type

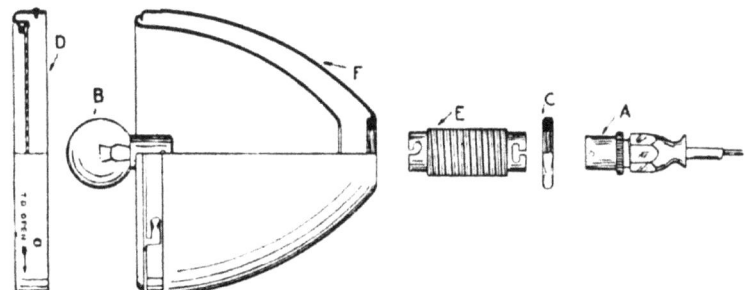

Fig. 69. Component Parts of Early Model Villiers Head Lamp

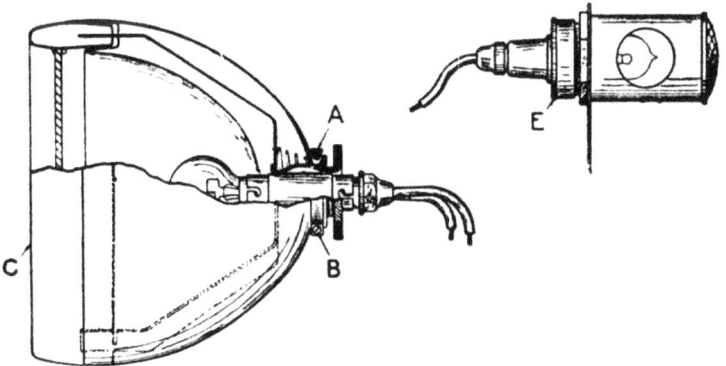

Fig. 70. Adjustment and Focusing of Early Large Model Head Lamp

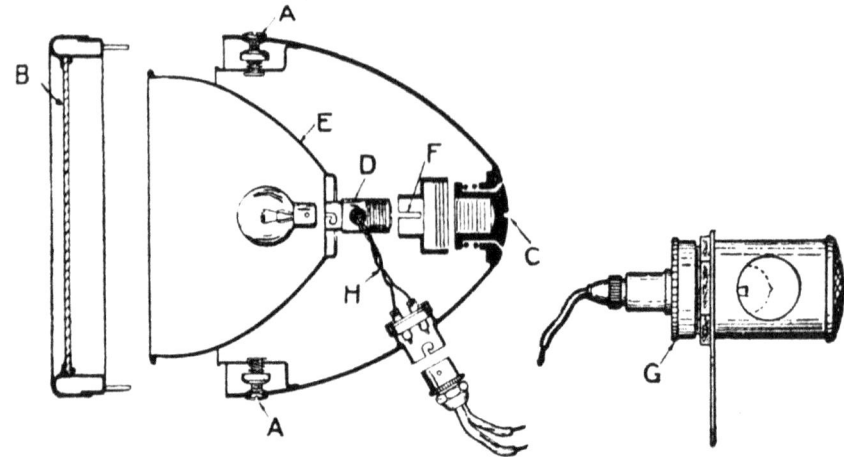

Fig. 71. Adjustment and Focusing of Early Model Head Lamp

Fig. 72. Tail Lamp

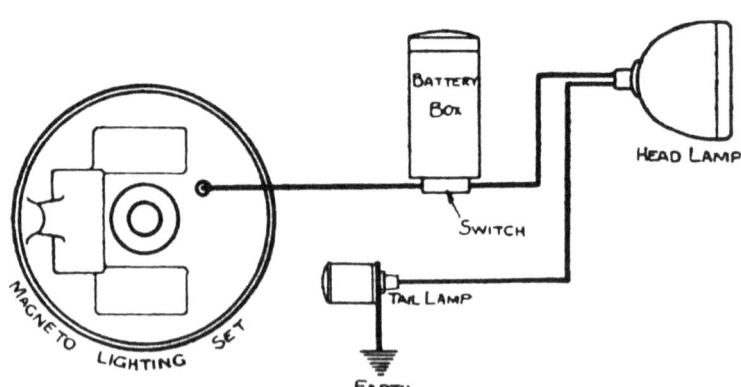

Fig. 73. Wiring Diagram of Old Type Direct Lighting Set with Stand-by Dry Battery

ELECTRIC LIGHTING SYSTEMS

its guide to obtain the correct focus, and then locked into position with the screw.

Tail Lamp. Fig. 72 shows this. The inside of the lamp may be withdrawn from the body by unscrewing the knurled cap G.

Owners of pre-war machines will be interested to know that the older model head and tail lamps can be converted to follow modern

Fig. 74. Split Terminal on Lighting Cable

practice and obtain the up-to-date benefits. It is as well to contact the makers direct giving full details.

The Dynamo Charging Set. This lighting set incorporates a Westinghouse metal rectifier under licence, and is a full accumulator set with none of the delicate parts, such as commutator, cut-outs, and slip-rings, which are necessary with the usual dynamo equipment. The wiring is quite straightforward, and as there are no moving parts, it is very unlikely for any trouble whatsoever to develop in this equipment. *On no account should the reader attempt to dismantle the rectifier, or to remove it from its case.*

The bulbs employed with this lighting set are 6 volt, 1 amp. gas filled for the head lamp; 6 volt, 3 amp. vacuum head lamp pilot bulb and 6 volt, 3 amp. vacuum tail lamp bulb, and for efficient results these should not be varied. The wiring of this set is shown in Fig. 78.

The following remarks are very important, and should be observed in the event of any difficulties.

1. *The rectifier must never be taken apart.*

This means that the nuts *A* and *B* (Fig. 78) must on no occasion be loosened, as this will destroy the necessary contact of the plates and reduce the efficiency of the rectifier.

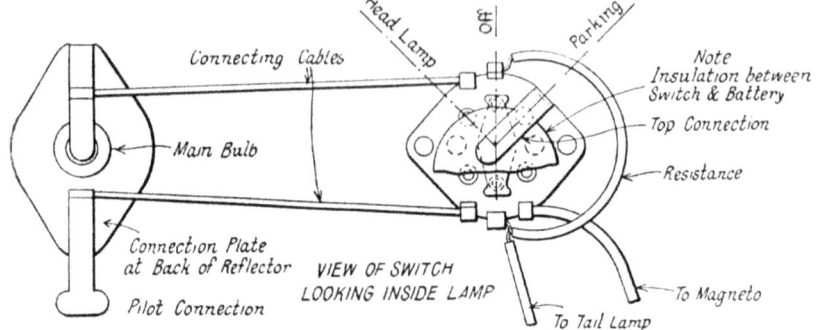

Fig. 75. Wiring Diagram for Villiers-auto Magneto Lighting (98 c.c. "Junior" Engine and Mark 2 F)

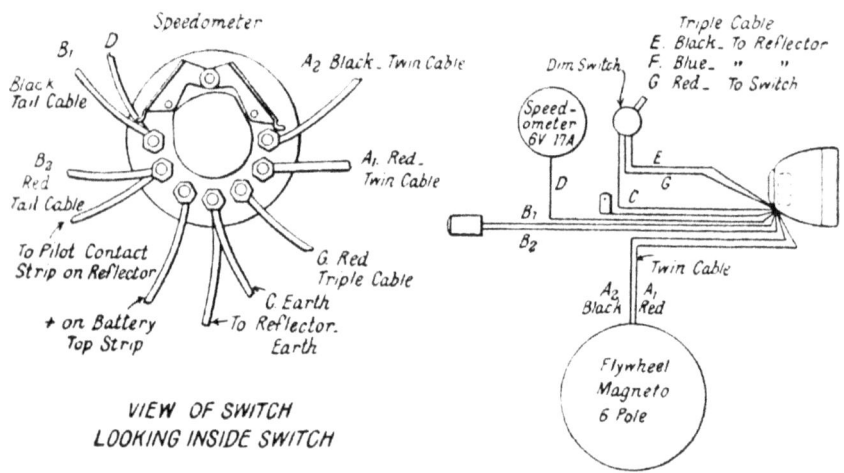

Fig. 76. Wiring Diagram for 6-Pole Magneto Set (125 c.c. "Unit" Engine)

2. It should never be necessary to remove the rectifier from its case.

3. Should it be required to remove the rectifier and case from the machine, the *positive* (+) terminal should be disconnected from the accumulator and the plunger terminals *X* and *Y* should be pulled out from the armature plate at the back of the fly-wheel magneto.

4. On no account must the engine be run when the accumulator

ELECTRIC LIGHTING SYSTEMS

has been removed and the rectifier is still in circuit. To prevent damage, pull out the two plunger terminals from the armature plates at the back of the fly-wheel magneto.

5. The plunger terminals X and Y must be pushed in their sockets as far as possible to make good contact.

6. The brackets C of the rectifier must make good contact with the frame of the machine.

7. Clean off all enamel where earth contacts are made.

8. The rectifier must not be fitted near the cylinder or in any other position where it will be subject to heat.

9. The rectifier must be kept dry, as oil or water between the fins will cause a short circuit.

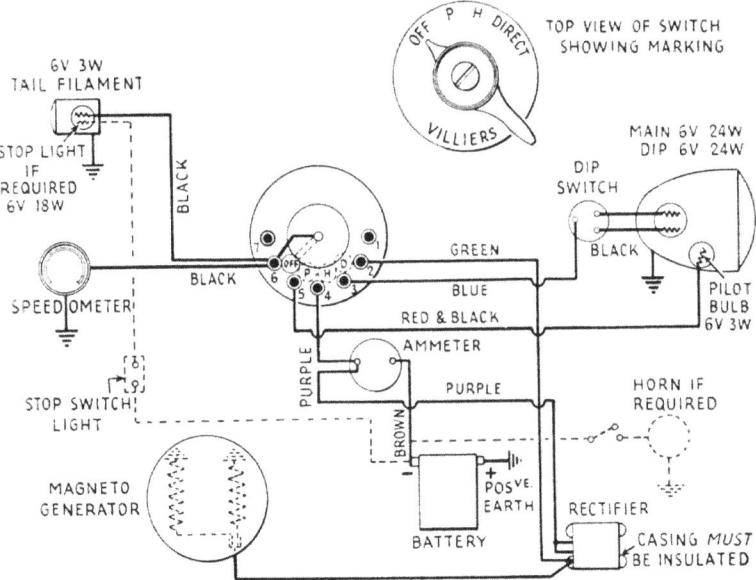

Fig. 77. Wiring Diagram for the "Rectifier" Lighting Set (Mark 10 D and Mark 6 E)

Head Lamp for Dynamo Charging Set. To remove front of the lamp A, Fig. 79, press in and twist in an anti-clockwise direction. The main bulb B is screwed into the coil of a spring D which holds it in any desired position. By this a very sensitive adjustment of the focus is obtained, as turning the bulb either to the right or left moves it backward or forward. The pilot bulb F is held in position by the usual bayonet clip, and the bulbs are connected by spring contact to the switch at the top of the lamp.

The knurled nuts X should not be removed or tightened.

The 2-Pole Magneto Lighting and Parking Set. For normal running the head lamp and tail lamp are lighted from the *coils* in the fly-wheel magneto, but a *dry battery* in a neat container is incorporated in the set, so that the rider may switch over when standing, and so obtain a light for parking. The equipment may be used in conjunction with the direct lighting coils in existing Villiers fly-wheel magnetos.

The 5½ in. and 7 in. head lamps have a neat three-way switch and are fitted with separate main and parking bulbs. The tail lamp

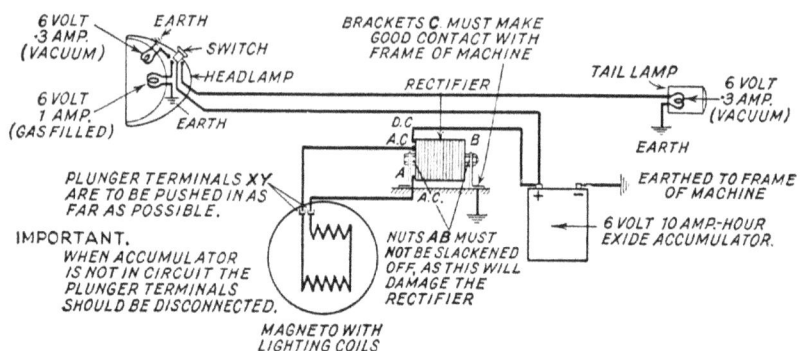

Fig. 78. Wiring Diagram for Dynamo Charging Set

is of improved design, and the correct bulbs employed in this lighting set are: 6 volt, 0·75 amp. for the head lamp bulb; 4 volt, 0·125 amp. for the head lamp parking bulb, and 6 volt, 0·3 amp. for the tail lamp bulb. The wiring of the set is shown in Fig. 80.

In the case of the 7 in. head lamps, if the switch is pressed over with too much force, it is just possible to break one of the internal stops which will allow the parking battery to make circuit with the magneto and thus cause demagnetization.

The 4-Pole Magneto Direct Lighting Set. It generates 70 per cent more light than in older models yet provides the same intense plug spark, and at such a low speed of even 10 miles per hour it definitely gives a brilliant light. It is so designed that it cannot burn out the bulbs.

This method is so simple that there are no moving parts except the fly-wheel and there is only one single cable to head and tail lamps.

The battery for the parking light is housed inside the head lamp and is thus watertight, safe, and secure. This battery and the bulbs are of standard pattern and obtainable at all shops and garages. A simple straightforward switch at the top of the lamp controls the light.

ELECTRIC LIGHTING SYSTEMS 101

Fig. 81 shows the housing of the dry battery in the 5½ in. headlamp, the fitting of the earth connexion (indicated by an arrow) and the correct position of the bulb holder. The main bulb

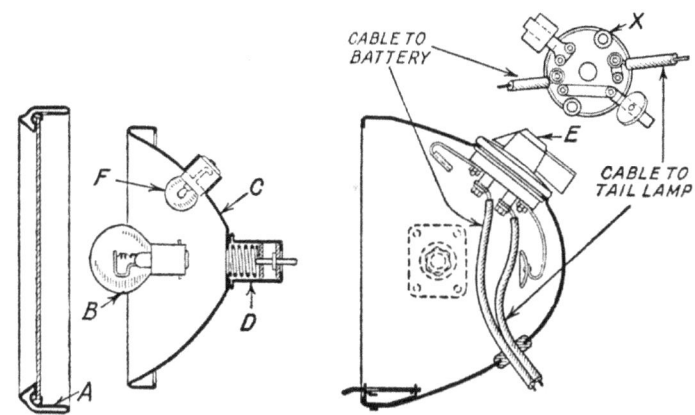

Fig. 79. Adjustment and Focusing Head Lamp (Dynamo Set)

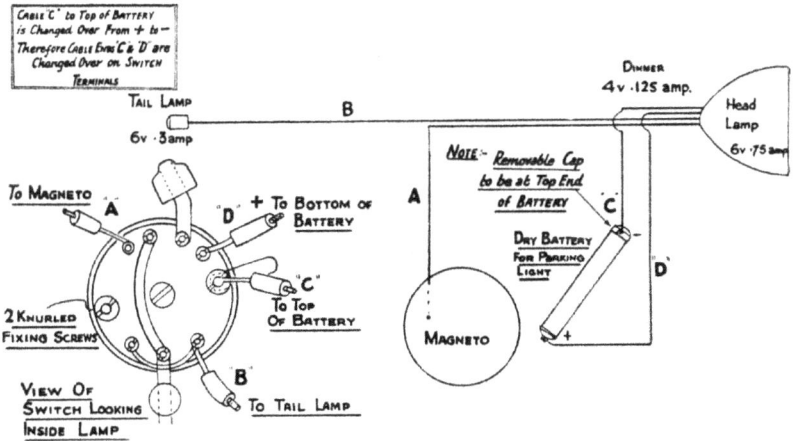

Fig. 80. Wiring Diagram for Old-type Parking Light Set

is 6 volt, 1 amp. gas filled, the pilot and tail bulbs being interchangeable, with a capacity of 3·5 volt, 0·3 amp. 7-in. head lamps were introduced later with double filament bulbs and handlebar dip-switch control.

All Villiers lighting sets are now obtainable with handlebar controlled dip switch, with the exception of the small lighting sets supplied for the Junior engine, and early pattern lighting sets for use with 2-pole fly-wheel magnetos.

102   THE BOOK OF THE VILLIERS

The 6-Pole Magneto Direct Lighting Set. Two types of 6-pole magneto are now available for fitting to the 125 c.c. engine Mark 9 D, the one generating sufficient current to light an 18-watt bulb in the head lamp and the other being suitable for a 24-watt head lamp bulb.

The tail lamp for both models is 6 watt. The lighting set employed is the 5½-in. set as already described.

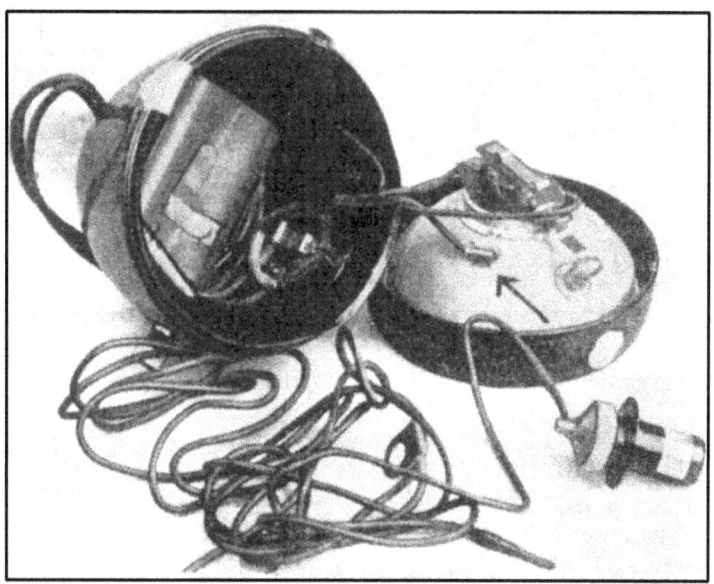

FIG. 81. SHOWING THE 5½ IN. HEAD LAMP USED WITH THE FOUR-POLE MAGNETO

Showing the housing of the parking dry battery, the fitting of the earth connexion (as at arrow), and the correct position of the bulb holder

Owing to the brilliant light, it is usual for a dip switch to be employed with this set, so that the rider can dim his light when approaching traffic.

A table of bulb sizes for the Villiers lighting sets is given in page 104, and this should be consulted for particulars of the correct bulbs to use with this equipment (for wiring diagram see page 98).

The 2-Pole Direct Lighting Set for the "Junior" Engine. On the autocycles using this engine a small specially designed lighting set is employed. The head lamp is of approximately 4 in. diameter, and a dry battery is neatly enclosed to provide a parking light when the engine is stationary. A three-way switch is fitted to the top of the headlamp and the tail lamp is included. A wiring diagram will be found on page 98.

ELECTRIC LIGHTING SYSTEMS

POST-WAR LIGHTING SYSTEMS

The 3-Pole Fly-wheel Magneto. This is fitted to Junior de-luxe engines and provides both ignition and lighting, the latter direct to the head lamp while the tail-lamp current is fed through a resistance so that a dry battery (Ever Ready No. 1289) can be used for parking purposes. The earth terminal is at the bottom of the lamp casing and it is therefore important that the lamp is in direct metallic contact with the cycle frame.

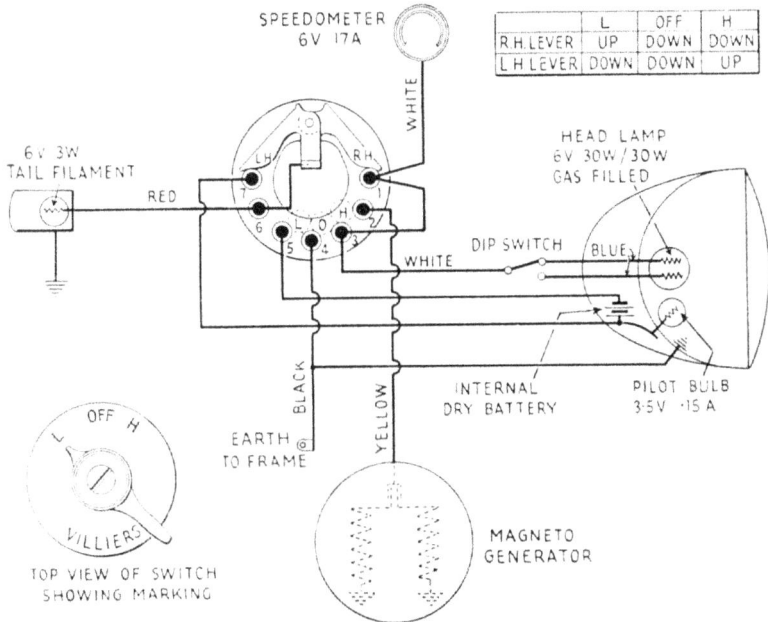

FIG. 82. WIRING DIAGRAM FOR THE "DIRECT" LIGHTING SET (MARK 10 D AND MARK 6 E)

The 6-Pole Fly-wheel Magneto. This fitted to the 98 c.c. Mark 1 F engine unit provides current for both ignition and lighting, the alternating current from the lighting coils being converted to direct current by passing through a fool-proof selenium type rectifier for charging a 6 volt 10 amp.-hour battery.

The 6-pole magneto fitted to the 125 c.c. Mark 10 D and 197 c.c. Mark 6 E engine-units can be used either for direct or rectifier lighting sets either of which is available at choice.

The wiring diagram for the "Rectifier" is shown on page 99.

LIST OF BULBS SUITABLE FOR VARIOUS VILLIERS LIGHTING SETS

Large 2-Pole Magneto (8¼ in. diam.)
Head lamp . 4 volt, 0·5 amp.   Double Contact
Tail lamp . 4 volt, 0·5 amp.   ,, ,,

Old Pattern Charging Set
Head lamp . 4 volt, 1 amp. gas-filled   ,, ,,
Tail lamp . 4 volt, 0·125 amp.   ,, ,,

Direct Lighting Set Less Parking Battery (Old Pattern 2-Pole Small Magneto, 7 in. diam.)
Head lamp . 6 volt, 0·5 amp. or 0·75 amp.   Double Contact
Tail lamp . 4 volt, 0·75 amp.   ,, ,,

Rectifier Charging Set
Head lamp . 6 volt, 1 amp. gas-filled.   Single Contact
Pilot . . 6 volt, 0·3 amp.   ,, ,,
Tail lamp . 6 volt, 0·3 amp.   ,, ,,

Small 2-Pole Magneto Direct Lighting Set with Parking Battery, 7 in. Lamp
Head lamp . 6 volt, 0·5 amp. or 0·75 amp.   ,, ,,
Pilot . . 4 volt, 0·125 amp.   ,, ,,
Tail lamp . 6 volt, 0·3 amp.   ,, ,,

Small 2-Pole Magneto Direct Lighting Set with Parking Battery, 5 in. Lamp
Head lamp . 6 volt, 0·5 amp.   ,, ,,
Tail lamp . 6 volt, 0·3 amp.   ,, ,,

4-Pole Magneto with Parking Battery, 5½ in. Lamp
Head lamp . 6 volt, 1 amp. gas-filled   ,, ,,
Pilot . . 3·5 volt, 0·3 amp.   ,, ,,
Tail lamp . 3·5 volt, 0·3 amp.   ,, ,,
    (WHERE SPEEDOMETER IS TO BE ILLUMINATED)
Head lamp . 6 volt, 1 amp. (no alteration)   ,, ,,
Pilot . . 3½ volt, 0·15 amp. (instead of 3½ volt, 0·3 amp.)   ,, ,,
Tail lamp . 3½ volt, 0·15 amp. (instead of 3½ volt, 0·3 amp.)   ,, ,,
Speedometer 3½ volt, 0·15 amp.   ,, ,,

4-Pole Magneto with Parking Battery, 7 in. Lamp
Head lamp . 6 volt, 1 amp. gas-filled   ,, ,,
Pilot . . 4 volt, 0·125 amp.   ,, ,,
Tail lamp . 6 volt, 0·3 amp.   ,, ,,
    (WHERE SPEEDOMETER IS TO BE ILLUMINATED)
Head lamp . 6 volt, 1 amp. (no alteration)   ,, ,,
Pilot . . 4 volt, 0·125 amp. (no alteration)   ,, ,,
Tail lamp . 4 volt, 0·125 amp. (instead of 6 volt 0·3 amp.)   ,, ,,
Speedometer 6 volt, 0·17 amp.   ,, ,,
    (FOR SETS WITH DIP SWITCH USE)
6 volt 6/6 watt   Double Contact

ELECTRIC LIGHTING SYSTEMS

2-Pole Magneto Fitted to the 125 c.c. Gear Unit Engines

Head lamp . 6 volt, 0·5 amp. — Single Contact
Pilot . . 3·5 volt, 0·3 amp. — ,, ,,
Tail lamp . 3·5 volt, 0·3 amp. — ,, ,,
(WHERE SPEEDOMETER IS TO BE ILLUMINATED)
Head lamp . 6 volt, 0·5 amp. (no alteration) — ,, ,,
Pilot . . 3½ volt, 0·15 amp. (instead of 3½ volt
    0·3 amp.) — ,, ,,
Tail lamp . 3½ volt, 0·15 amp. (instead of 3½ volt
    0·3 amp.) — ,, ,,
Speedometer 3½ volt, 0·15 amp. — ,, ,,

6-Pole Magneto for 5½ in. and 7 in. Lamps

For the 18 watt Lighting Set.
Head lamp . 6 volt, 18/18 watt double filament — Double Contact
For the 24 watt Lighting Set.
Head lamp . 6 volt, 24/24 watt double filament — Double Contact
For both 18 watt and 24 watt Lighting Sets.
Pilot lamp . 3½ volt, 0·15 amp. — Single Contact
Tail lamp . 6 volt, 6 watt/3·5 volt 0·3 amp. double fil. — Double Contact
Speedometer. 6 volt, 0·17 amp. — Single Contact

2-Pole Magneto on Junior Engines

Head lamp . 6 volt, 0·5 amp. — Single Contact
Pilot lamp . 4 volt, 0·3 amp. — ,, ,,
Tail lamp . 3·5 volt, 0·3 amp. — ,, ,,

3-Pole Magneto on Junior De-luxe Engines with Separate Main and Parking Bulbs

Head lamp . 6 volt, 1 amp. — Single Contact
Pilot lamp . 4 volt, 0·3 amp — ,, ,,
Tail lamp . 4 volt, 0·3 amp. — ,, ,,

With one bulb for main and parking
Head lamp . 6 volt, 1 amp. — Single Contact
Tail lamp . 4 volt, 0·3 amp. — ,, ,,

Magneto Lighting Sets. These are used in conjunction with the fly-wheel-magneto generators on all current models. The sets are available for both rectifier and direct lighting and are complete with head and tail lamps, wiring harness, switch and ammeter (where required).

CHAPTER IX
THREE-WHEELED CARS

THERE has never been cheaper, safer and more comfortable motoring than has been made possible by the introduction of three-wheeled cars fitted with Villiers engines. They have now proved their value over millions of miles and apart from extreme economy they do offer motor-car comfort at motor-cycle cost.

At the moment of going to press there are three different makes, namely the Bond Minicar, the A.C. "Petite" and the Gordon.

THE BOND MINICAR

The striking feature is that it has been designed and built for two adults and three children with full weather protection for all and at a total running cost of less than 1d. per mile, petrol consumption being from 85 to 90 miles to the gallon. But this does not mean that the speed is low because it is quite easy to cruise at 40 m.p.h. even with a head wind, while the maximum speed is nearer 50 m.p.h. At the same time the car is safe because of the efficient internally expanding brakes which are mechanically operated, the front by rod and cable and the rear by rods.

Comfort. The excellent suspension sees to this. The front wheel is mounted on a trailing arm suspended by double acting hydraulic shock absorbers around which is a coil spring, while the rear is by trailing arms on independent bonded rubber units which require no maintenance. The ability of these modern three wheelers to hold the road is extraordinary.

Comfort is also ensured by the quality of the upholstery, and by the bench-type seat and squab on spring cages lined with Dunlopillo and covered with ribbed Vynide. It is not necessary, even, to get out to start the engine because starting is performed manually from the driving seat, and a quick start is assured by the use of the automatic decompressor. A self starter is fitted on the Mark D de Luxe.

Weather Protection. The hood and side screens are so designed that there is full weather protection and yet at the same time ample viewing space all round. The hood is of unshrinkable Vynide which is held secure by thumb screws but easily raised and lowered. The side screens are stored in special clips. Whether the hood is up or down the appearance is essentially neat.

Bodywork. The appearance is modern and streamlined. The body is made of aluminium alloy and steel, with a cast-aluminium bulk-head on the stressed skin principle, with the bonnet and rear wings in the modern Fibreglass plastic to reduce the chance of denting. Exposed metal parts are stove-enamelled. It requires little space for garaging, Marks C and D being 9 ft 10 in. long, 4 ft 9 in. wide, 4 ft high, having a ground clearance of 7 in. and

Fig. 83. The Bond Minicar

weighing 470 lb. The "New Bond" is 11 ft long, 4 ft 7 in. wide, has a ground clearance of 7 in. and weighs 620 lb.

Steering gives 90 degrees lock both sides so that the car can be turned round in its own diagonal length, and is by worm and sector and easily adjustable for wear.

The Mechanical Aspect. Mark C has the famous 197 c.c. Villiers engine Mark 8 E with 3-speed gear unit with ratios 1, 1·7, and 3·25 to 1, with an output of 8 b.h.p. The Mark D and New Bond are powered by the 197 c.c. Villiers engine Mark 9 E, with 3-speed gear unit giving an output of 8·5 b.h.p. No reverse gear is necessary because of the steering lock of 180 degrees.

Transmission is by roller chain to the front wheel sprockets, adjustments being quite simple by a new type of screw in two or three minutes. All wheels are interchangeable and carry 4·00 × 8 low pressure tyres. The 2½ gallon tank in the Mark C and 3½ gallon tank in the New Bond are mounted in the bulk-head and are fed via a flexible pipe by gravity to the carburettor. There is also a reserve controlled by a separate tap which provides ample petrol for a further 15 miles.

The electrical equipment is especially complete with a 6-volt battery, Mark C, and 12 volt Mark D and New Bond, charged through a rectifier from the fly-wheel magneto-dynamo giving an output of 7 amps, and amply sufficient for controlling the head and side lamps, rear and braking lights, dash light, electric wiper, dip switch, reflectors and horn.

As for carrying luggage there is surprising accommodation at the rear of the seat, while the tool-kit is carried beneath the seat or, if you wish, in the luggage boot.

Ease of Maintenance. What appeals possibly to the economically minded is the ease and low cost of maintenance. There are, for instance, only 8 greasing points and 9 oiling points, while the entire power unit and transmission can be dropped out by removing only 5 bolts and 4 cables. For anybody mechanically minded the Bond Minicar need never go into a garage.

Reliability, however, has been proved over and over again, especially in the gruelling 2,000-mile route of the Monte Carlo rally where it proved to be fully capable of maintaining a steady course over roads covered with black ice and snow.

Practical Help. It is most essential to carry out the running-in instructions and it is preferable to add a little extra oil to the petrol-oil mixture for 200 miles. If you want a long lasting and efficient engine, then the car should not be driven in excess of 10 m.p.h. in first gear, 15 m.p.h in second gear and 25 m.p.h. in third gear for 500 miles. Neither should one expect full power until 1,000 miles has been covered. Coasting downhill is never good practice whether this is done by putting the gear into neutral or by holding the clutch pedal depressed.

Another point is to check the nuts and bolts on the engine and gear-box unit, road wheels and body fittings for tightness and of course tyre pressures (28 lb. per sq. in front, 22 lb. per sq. in. rear).

If these light cars are to retain their comfort and give trouble-free service, then the instructions for lubrication and maintenance as given in the book should be followed through, and it is well to keep a log book of the work carried out whether daily or weekly.

THE A.C. "PETITE" MARK II

Here we have a light car which in several features differs from other cars of this type. Firstly, there is a much greater power in the 346 c.c. engine, giving a maximum output of 8·25 b.h.p. at 3,500 r.p.m. The engine is mounted in the rear, which allows for a surprising amount of leg room and a comfortable bench-type seat with luggage area behind. It is easy to approach for adjustment. It has the famous Villiers fly-wheel magneto with a large cooling fan. The gear-box provides three forward ratios of 4·85, 8·95, and 18·95 to 1, and one reverse.

THREE-WHEELED CARS

The Transmission. The transmission is by triple vee-belt, which proves surprisingly quiet and gives a fine cushioning effect, with multi-plate clutch on the gear-box and with final drive to a differential by chain. To follow orthodox big car practice the rear axle has a separate differential assembly with two open half shafts incorporating double Hardy Spicer universal joints.

Brakes and Suspension. The brakes are Girling with 7-in. drums on both rear wheels which carry tyres of 4.00×12. Each

Fig. 84. The A.C. "Petite"

wheel is independently sprung, the single front wheel having two coil springs controlled by dampers and the rear wheels also with coil springs with the compression controlled by direct action tubular hydraulic dampers attached to each trailing arm. The wheel base is 6 ft., the track 4 ft. and ground clearance $6\frac{3}{4}$ in.

Under the worst road conditions the independent springing gives absolute comfort and stability, the hydraulic brakes give full control even in surprised circumstances, while the steering column gear-change makes driving simple and certain.

Electrical Equipment. The Petite has a 12-volt Lucas electric dynamo system and starter, a double dip to both headlamps, separate side lamps and a tail lamp incorporating a brake stoplight. The wiper and horn are electrically operated.

Controls. The clutch, brake and accelerator pedal are precisely like those on a standard car and the hand brake is of the pistol type.

Bodywork. Perhaps the body comes in for special notice because it is of the fully-built saloon type, with a toughened glass windscreen and with vertical sliding door glasses. The hood rolls down between the main pillars of the saloon head. There are two doors

Fig. 85. The Engine Assembly of the A.C. "Petite"

and the body itself is made of strong aluminium panelling with upholstery in plastic on padded spring cases.

The overall length of the car is 10 ft. 3 in., the width 4 ft. 7 in., and the height 4 ft. 7 in. with a total weight of only $7\frac{1}{2}$ cwt.

The chassis and body frame are integral light gauge steel of generous section for strength and lightness. The engine, gearbox and differential are rubber mounted for quietness.

It will be seen that this car is of the luxury type and whilst naturally more expensive than the less highly powered cars it nevertheless does 60 to 70 miles to the gallon, cruises at 40 with a maximum of 50 m.p.h. and a road tax of £5 and an insurance of £8. Because of its complete weather defying build it is claimed that a garage is not essential. It is not a toy but, the makers claim, a real "life size" car which will do most of that which its

THREE-WHEELED CARS

larger brothers can do and at considerably lower cost and that it is "made a little better than it need be."

It needs little room for parking, is simple to maintain, easy to handle, and has such a low petrol consumption that it costs less than 1½d. a mile to run including insurance and tax. Wives use it for taking their children to school or for shopping while the husband, to cut costs, finds it valuable for travelling to work or for use for holidays, week-end trips or for professional visits.

There is ample seating for two plus a child, still leaving space for luggage.

The fuel is oil and petrol to the ratio of 1 to 20. Much of the future value will be obtained by running in carefully as the manufacturers advise in their leaflet. Attention must be given to the petrol-oil filter, and air filter, to the cleanliness of the sparking plug, and to the contact breaker points. There is little to go wrong and if the operating instructions are studied and the engine treated intelligently many years of happy and carefree motoring can be expected.

THE GORDON FAMILY CAR

Here again is a lightweight three-wheeled car which the family man with one or two children and limited means can afford to buy and run.

Mechanical Specification. It makes use of the Villiers Mark S E/R engine of 197 c.c. giving a maximum b.h.p. of 8 at 4,500 r.p.m. This engine-gear unit has three forward gears and a reverse, is fan-cooled and has an electric starter.

The engine and gear-box are mounted in a unique fashion on the offside of the car on a Metalastik mounting covered with a clip-fastened cowl which gives unobstructed quick access to the engine so that maintenance and servicing are easy.

The drive from the engine to the gear-box is by a ⅜ in. pitch chain while the gear-box ratios are 7·76, 10·84, and 17·85 to 1.

The overall length is 10 ft. 2 in., the width 4 ft. 9½ in., the height with hood up 4 ft. 7½ in., the ground clearance 6 in. and the weight 6 cwt. 44 lb.

All wheels and tyres are interchangeable and the spare wheel is carried in the boot. Tyre sizes are 5·20 × 15 with a front pressure of 18 lb. per sq. in. and the rear of 20 lb. per sq. in.

The Electrical Equipment. A 6 volt 57 amp battery charged from the fly-wheel magneto-dynamo through a rectifier is fitted, and there are two head lamps, two stop lights, two side lamps and two tail lamps.

Fig. 86. The Gordon Three-wheeled Car Showing Engine Mounting

Fig. 87. The Gordon Three-wheeled Car Showing Ease of Accessibility

THREE-WHEELED CARS

Controls. Control is definite and easy through a spring steering wheel, quadrant gear-change by lever mounted on the right hand with foot brake, clutch and accelerator pedal as in ordinary car practice. The hand brake operates on the front wheel and the lever is mounted under the dash, giving two independent braking systems, while steering is by means of the Burman steering unit.

Suspension and Brakes. The rear wheels are independently sprung on coil springs while the front wheel is on Metalastik torsion bushes. Brakes with drums of malleable casting 7 in. in diameter, work on all three wheels and are operated by Bowden cables. The hand brake acts on the front wheel.

Bodywork. The body is of the open touring type but good protection is afforded by a hood of beige proofed cloth on a stove-enamel frame with plastic back and side lights along with five curtains. Windscreens are of polished aluminium, glazed with toughened plate glass.

Seating is of the bench type covered with plastic upholstery on padded spring cases. There is a particularly large luggage boot 34 in. × 24 in. × 18 in.

It is reckoned that the Gordon is able to give 70 to 80 miles to the gallon with a maximum speed of 45 m.p.h. and costs less than $\frac{3}{4}$d. a mile to run.

Running In. If the owner wishes to make sure of a long life for the engine, then he must take special care with regard to running in, and during the first 500 miles he should not drive in excess of 10 m.p.h. in first gear, 15 m.p.h. in second and 25 m.p.h. in third; neither should he coast with the clutch out or in neutral.

Maintenance. Maintenance is of a simple order and, if the instruction book is studied, most of the jobs including overhaul can be done by an intelligent owner. Wheels can be changed easily, decarbonizing is a simple operation and adjustment of clutch, magneto, carburettor and brakes is easily understood and carried through.

Dipping head lights, toughened glass windscreen, electric starter, independent suspension on all wheels, three forward gears and reverse, and internal expanding brakes are features found on the more expensive cars which go to make this light car of outstanding value.

APPENDIX A

1959 SUPPLEMENT

ADDITIONAL VILLIERS MOTOR-CYCLE ENGINES

DESCRIBED below are the Villiers motor-cycle engines recently introduced and which are not specifically dealt with in earlier chapters of this book. General principles of maintenance and overhaul already described apply, but mention will be made of any special points regarding maintenance relevant to the units dealt with in the following paragraphs.

The 50 c.c. Mark 3 K. This is a two-speed engine-gear unit designed as a power unit for mopeds. With a cast-iron cylinder and light-alloy cylinder head, the motor has a bore of 40 mm. and a stroke of 39·7 mm. giving a swept volume of 50 c.c. The compression ratio is 7 to 1 and the power output 2 b.h.p. at 5,500 r.p.m., which enables the motor to drive a typical moped at speeds of up to 30 m.p.h. The unit is fitted with pedal cranks, by which means the motor is started and which enable the machine to be pedalled with the motor out of action. The pedalling gear incorporates a back-pedalling brake mechanism.

The piston has two rings and the gudgeon pin is located by circlips. The small end is bushed while the big-end bearing consists of 24 $\frac{3}{16} \times \frac{3}{16}$ in. rollers. The mainshafts run on ball bearings, and the motor transmits its power via a mainshaft-mounted clutch and chain to a sprocket splined to the gear cluster in the gear-box and retained by a nut. The gear cluster runs in a ball-bearing housed in the right-hand crankcase half and is bushed internally to run on the pedal shaft which also carries the pedal ratchet mechanism. In constant mesh with this gear cluster are the countershaft pinions which run free on the countershaft. The gear selector is located between these pinions, and moves laterally on splines on the countershaft. The gear selector can lock either pinion to the countershaft to give the required gear ratio. The selector is cable-operated from the handlebar, and the internal gear ratios are 1 to 3·06 and 1 to 1·71. At its left-hand end the pedal shaft runs in a bush housed in the left-hand crankcase half, while the countershaft runs in a bush at its right-hand end and on 12 $\frac{3}{16} \times \frac{3}{16}$ in. rollers at the other. The final-drive sprocket is keyed to the countershaft.

A Villiers SM 10 carburettor is fitted which incorporates a stream-lined detachable air filter. Current for lighting and ignition is provided by a Villiers flywheel-magneto, the lighting output being 6 volts, 18 watts. Ignition timing advance is $\frac{3}{32}$ in. before top-dead-centre. The recommended sparking plug is a Lodge BN 14 mm.

Maintenance of this unit is simple, and general instructions given elsewhere in the book apply. The petrol/oil ratio is 24 to 1 of SAE 30 oil. SAE 30 oil is also recommended for the gearbox, the capacity of which is $\frac{5}{8}$ pint. The gearbox oil-level should be checked every 500 miles by removing the level plug on the right-hand (i.e. transmission) side beneath the front of the crankcase. The drain plug is on the left-hand side and the filler plug is on top of the crankcase to the left and behind the cylinder. The vent hole in this plug must be kept clear. It is recommended that the gear-box be drained completely and refilled every 1,000 miles.

Maintaining the flywheel-magneto is simply a matter of inspecting the contact-breaker points every 2,000 miles and cleaning and adjusting them if necessary. To gain access to the magneto the left-hand pedal crank and crankcase half must be removed. Adjustment of the contact-breaker points can be made through one of the apertures in the flywheel. The correct gap is 0·012 in.–0·015 in. and should be checked with a feeler gauge. To alter the gap, the bracket-retaining screw must be slackened and the smaller adjusting screw turned in the appropriate direction. The bracket-retaining screw must, of course, be retightened when the adjustment has been made. Cleaning the contact-breaker points can best be done with a petrol-moistened rag. Cleaning of the sparking plug should be carried out every 500 miles and, at the same time the gap re-adjusted to 0·018in.–0·022 in.

The carburettor air filter should be cleaned by swilling in neat petrol at about 2,000-mile intervals, the filter being dipped in petroil mixture and allowed to drain before being refitted. Care should be taken to see that the sealing ring between carburettor and filter is correctly replaced.

The clutch will need adjustment from time to time. This adjustment is made by turning the nut on the end of the clutch which is reached through the aperture sealed by a plug in the right-hand crankcase cover. The nut should be turned in a clockwise direction until the clutch can be just made to slip by turning the pedal against engine compression. The slack in the operating cable should then be taken up completely and the adjusting screw turned anti-clockwise one-quarter of a turn. The clutch cable should then be readjusted so that there is $\frac{1}{8}$ in. free movement. The gear-change cable adjustment is correct when the cable is slightly slack with top gear engaged.

APPENDIX A

The 148 c.c. Mark 31 C. This is the latest model of a well-tried design with a bore of 57 mm. and a stroke of 58 mm., a compression ratio of 7·75 to 1, and with a choice of the 3-speed (Mark 31 C/3) gear-box (Ratios 1, 1·34 and 2·55 to 1) or 4-speed (Mark 31 C/4) gear-box (1, 1·27, 1·78 and 2·94 to 1) integral with the engine.

It has a detachable aluminium-alloy cylinder-head fitted to a cast iron cylinder with the modern arrangement of one inlet, one exhaust, and two transfer ports, and an aluminium flat-topped, two-ring piston.

The carburettor is the type S.19 with the new design of oil-wetted air filter incorporating an air strangler for easy starting; ignition is by totally-enclosed fly-wheel magneto. The weight overall is about 63 lb. A speedometer drive can be fitted at the time of ordering. The fuel consumption of this engine is 100 m.p.g.

The 173 c.c. Mark 2 L. Another new type which is similar in many respects to the Mark 9 E from which it was, in fact, derived, the main difference being the shorter stroke of the 2 L. The bore is 59 mm., stroke 63·5 mm., and compression ratio 7·4 to 1. The type S.22 carburettor is fitted. The weight is about 67 lb. A speedometer drive can be fitted at the time of ordering. The fuel consumption is 110 m.p.g.

The 197 c.c. 9 E Trials and Sports Model. This is a special unit with a heavier fly-wheel for smooth torque at low engine-speeds. It also has a special high-tension coil and contact-breaker arm, a high-compression head (compression ratio 8·25 to 1) fitted with a compression-release valve, and a new "1100" air cleaner. The 3-speed gear-box ratios are 1, 1·7, and 3·25 to 1, and the 4-speed, 1, 1·34, 2·4, and 3·6 to 1.

The 197 c.c. Mark 9 E. This was developed from the Mark 8 E with the same bore and stroke and a compression ratio of 7·25 to 1. It is popular for use in 3-wheeled cars. The general specification is similar to Mark 8 E (page 19). The 3-speed gear-box ratios (Mark 9 E/3) are 1, 1·34 and 2·55 to 1, and the 4-speed ratios (Mark 9 E/4) are 1, 1·27, 1·78, and 2·94 to 1. The weight is about 67 lb. This unit can be fitted at the time of ordering with a speedometer drive operating from the gear-box layshaft. The fuel consumption is 85 m.p.g.

The 246 c.c. 2 H Engine. This unit is a development of the 224 c.c. 1 H unit, and in fact the specifications of the two are identical, apart from the greater cubic capacity of the 2 H engine which has been obtained by increasing the bore measurement to

66 mm. The compression ratio is 7·25 to 1 and the engine produces 11·5 b.h.p. at 4,750 r.p.m. The gear-box and fly-wheel magnets are the same as those on the 1 H unit. The clutch assembly has been modified and "Neolangite" replaces the cork formerly employed as friction material. Nine springs located in a housing supersede the earlier double-coil compression spring and the chain wheel now runs on $24\frac{3}{16}$-in. diameter rollers instead of a ball-bearing assembly as before. A Villiers S.25/5 carburettor is fitted and a detail of styling which distinguishes the 2 H is that the cylinder is inclined slightly towards the front.

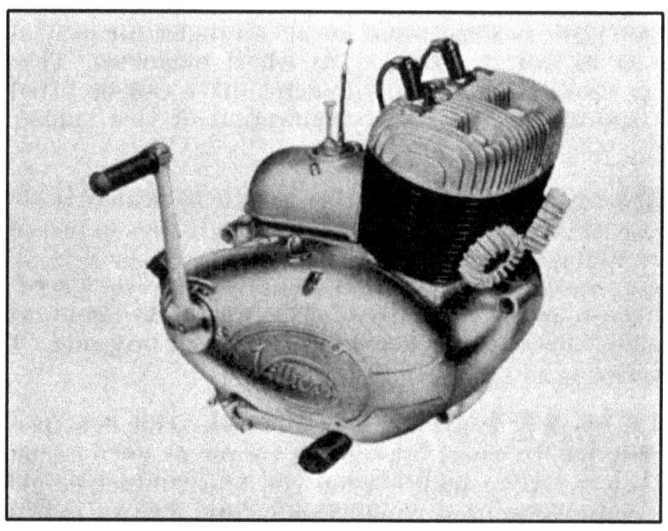

FIG. 87. THE 249 C.C. MARK 2 T ENGINE

The 249 c.c. Twin-cylinder 2 T Engine. The 2 T engine consists, in effect, of two single-cylinder engines assembled side by side with crankshafts coupled to give 180-degree firing intervals. The centre main bearing (a roller bearing) and oil seal are housed in a circular centre-plate, while a ball bearing and a roller bearing support the built-up crankshaft on drive side and generator side respectively. The lubrication of the main bearings is supplemented by oil drain holes in the crankcase. Roller-bearing big-ends are employed, the small-ends having steel-backed bronze bushes. The solid-skirt, flat-topped pistons each have two rings, the lower ones having expanders fitted behind them and, in consistency with Villiers practice, the gudgeon-pin bosses are bronze-bushed. The separate light-alloy cylinder-heads have half-pear shaped combustion chambers, and the compression ratio is 7·25 to 1. Bore and stroke measurements for this engine, which is stated to produce 15·0 b.h.p. at 5,500 r.p.m., are 50 mm. and 63·5 mm. respectively, and primary drive and clutch are as for the 2 H. The gear-box internal ratios are 1, 1·32, 1·9 and 3·06 to 1. Ignition arrangements include twin contact-breakers and H.T. coils in conjunction with the fly-wheel generator which also provides lighting current. A Villiers S.22/2 carburettor is fitted, and the complete 2 T unit weighs 94 lb.

The 324 c.c. Twin-cylinder Engine. This unit is basically the same as the 2 T. An increase in bore size to 57 mm. however, gives the greater capacity and an increase in power to 16·5 b.h.p. at 5,000 r.p.m. the stroke and the compression ratio being the same as for the 2 T. The 3 T has a 25-tooth engine sprocket, compared with the 20-tooth sprocket of the 2 T, and the gear-box ratios are 1 to 1, 1·55 to 1, 2·22 to 1, and 4·1 to 1. A Villiers S. 25/3 carburettor is fitted, having a No. 3 throttle and a No. $3\frac{1}{2}$ taper needle. As with the 2 T, ignition is by twin coils and contact breakers, the timing advance being $\frac{3}{16}$ in. before top dead centre. The correct contact-breaker points gap is 0·020 in.– 0·022 in. The total weight of the unit is 125 lb.

Instructions for decarbonizing were given in Chapter V. With later units, however, an expander ring is fitted behind the lower piston ring and serves to prevent noise caused by piston slap when the motor is cold. It is recommended that this expander ring be renewed whenever decarbonizing is undertaken, since it will, by then, have lost some of its temper and effectiveness.

For all the above mentioned units SAE 30 oil is recommended for the gearbox, and SAE 20 oil for the primary chaincase. The primary drive is by pre-stretched chain, so that maintenance is confined to keeping the oil at the correct level and the clutch in adjustment. With regard to the latter, the clutch push-rod should protrude from the gearbox casing by $\frac{5}{16}$ in. Adjustment is effected by turning the screw in the clutch-cap nut. The screw should be secured by its locking nut after the adjustment has been made. There should also be $\frac{1}{16}$ in. free play before the clutch-operating arm starts to compress the clutch springs by bearing on the end of the push rod. This adjustment must be made with the clutch cable slackened off.

The Villiers flywheel magneto fitted to these units consists of an armature plate on which are mounted the lighting and ignition coils, a flywheel containing the magnets and keyed to the engine shaft, and the contact-breaker mechanism which is housed in a compartment in the crankcase cover, the operating cam being keyed to the extension of the engine shaft. The crankcase cover encloses the complete assembly and access to the contact-breaker mechanism is gained by removing a small plate on the side of the cover. With regard to the 2 T twin-cylinder units the ignition timing of each cylinder must be dealt with separately. Should the need for adjustment arise, the contact-breaker base-plate screws which are secured by solder should be released and, with the contact points correctly gapped, the appropriate piston should be moved to the correct point in its travel. Then the appropriate base plate should be moved until the contact-breaker points are just on the point of opening. The base plate should then be firmly secured and the process repeated for the other cylinder. It is recommended that the cam-lubricating pad be soaked occasionally in high-melting-point grease heated to make it sufficiently fluid. On the 3 T the contact-breaker base plate is in one piece, so that when one cylinder has been correctly timed, the other is also automatically correct.

The Siba Dynastart. Certain of the above units can be fitted with this component which, while performing the duties of the normal flywheel magneto, serves also, in conjunction with a battery, as a starter motor. The system in this case is 12-volt D.C. Where the engine is fitted to a light car, the Dynastart can incorporate reverse starting. One advantage of the two-stroke engine is that it will run in reverse, thus avoiding the need for a reverse gear in the gearbox. The motor must be stopped before the reverse mechanism is operated, and it is recommended that only first gear be used when driving in reverse. About every 5,000 miles the rotor of the Dynastart should be removed and the commutator and brushes cleaned.

APPENDIX B

USEFUL INFORMATION

TABLE OF GRADIENTS

Gradient	Per cent	No. of feet rise or fall in 1 mile
1 in 2	50	2640
1 ,, 2½	40	2112
1 ,, 3	34	1760
1 ,, 3½	28	1508
1 ,, 4	25	1320
1 ,, 5	20	1056
1 ,, 6	17	880
1 ,, 7	14	754
1 ,, 8	12½	660
1 ,, 9	11	587
1 ,, 10	10	528
1 ,, 11	9	480
1 ,, 12	8	440
1 ,, 13	7¾	406
1 ,, 14	7	377
1 ,, 15	6½	352
1 ,, 16	6¼	330
1 ,, 17	6	311
1 ,, 18	5½	293
1 ,, 19	5	278
1 ,, 20	5	264
1 ,, 25	4	211
1 ,, 30	3·3	176
1 ,, 35	2·8	154
1 ,, 40	2½	132

EQUIVALENT SPEEDS

Speeds in m.p.h.	Time taken to cover 1 mile
10	6 minutes
15	4 ,,
20	3 ,,
25	2 ,, 24 seconds
30	2 ,,
35	1 ,, 42$\frac{6}{7}$,,
40	1 ,, 30 ,,
50	1 ,, 12 ,,
60	1 ,,

APPROXIMATE ENGINE REVOLUTIONS

At Different Speeds—Miles Per Hour

Gear Ratio	4	4¼	4½	4¾	5	5¼	5½	5¾	6	6¼	6½	6¾	7
Speed in Miles Hour													
5	260	276	292	309	325	346	358	374	388	404	420	437	453
10	520	552	584	618	650	692	716	748	775	808	840	875	905
15	780	828	876	927	975	1038	1074	1122	1160	1210	1260	1310	1360
20	1040	1104	1168	1236	1300	1384	1432	1496	1550	1615	1680	1750	1810
25	1300	1380	1460	1545	1625	1730	1790	1870	1940	2020	2100	2180	2265
30	1560	1656	1752	1854	1950	2076	2148	2244	2320	2420	2520	2620	2720
35	1820	1932	2044	2163	2275	2422	2506	2618	2710	2830	2950	3060	3170
40	2080	2208	2336	2472	2600	2768	2864	2992	3100	3230	3370	3490	3620
45	2340	2484	2628	2781	2925	3114	3222	3366	3490	3640	3790	3940	4070
50	2600	2760	2920	3090	3250	3460	3580	3740	3880	4040	4310	4370	4530
55	2860	3036	3212	3399	3575	3806	3938	4114	4270	4440	4630	4800	4980
60	3120	3312	3504	3709	3900	4152	4296	4488	4650	4850	5040	5240	5440

Diameter of Driving Wheels, 26 in.
For 24 in. Wheels, multiply revolutions by 1·08.   For 28 in. Wheels multiply by 0·93.

INDEX

A.C. "Petite" car 108
Accumulator lighting set, 92
Air cleaner, 87
Armature, 65
—— plate, 69
Automatic lubrication system, 34

BOND Minicar, 106
Bulbs, list of, 104
Bushes and bearings, 62

CARBON removal, 52
Carburettor, 77
—— construction, 78
—— dismantling, 84
—— setting, 81
—— tuning, 81
Chains and chain sprockets, 61
Cleaning engine, 46
Coasting, 42
Condenser, 65
Connecting rod, 1, 2, 31
Contact breaker, 66, 72
—— points adjusting, 72
Controls, 38
Crankcase assembly, 60
Crankshaft assembly, 2, 31
Cycle of operations, 4
Cylinder removal, 47
—— wear, 59

DATA, road performances, etc., 30
Decarbonizing, 53
Direct Lighting Set, 92
Dismantling carburettor, 84
—— engine, 47
Dynamo charging set, 97, 100, 102

ELECTRIC lighting systems, 92
Engine, cleaning, 46
——, how to handle, 38
—— troubles, 42
Exhaust pipe, cleaning, 61

FAULT-FINDING charts, 43
Fly-wheel magneto, 65

Focusing lamps, 94
—— types, 76
Four stroking, 41

GEAR-BOX, use of, 40
Gordon car, 111
Gradients, table of, 121
Gudgeon pin, 31

HEAVYWEIGHT carburettor, 90

IGNITION control, 41
—— retarded, 73
Inertia ring, 31

JET sizes, 81
Junior carburettor, 89

LAMPS, 94
Lighting systems, 92
Lubrication, 32, 72

MAGNETO, dismantling, 69
——, principle of, 65
——, refitting, 71
——, types, 76
Midget carburettor, 87
Minicar, the Bond, 106

NEEDLE changing, 82
—— sizes, 81
Noises, significance of, 41

OIL consumption, 30
—— supply adjustment, 37
Overhauling, 46

PETROIL system, 33
Petrol consumption of models, 30
Piston, 1, 29
——, removal of, 48
——, ring grooves, 56
——, rings, 51
Plugs, sparking, 74
Ports, cylinder, 56

Post-war lighting systems, 103
Principal components described, 29

REAR lamp, 92
Reassembling, 60
Release valve, 57
Retarded ignition, 69
Road performances, data, 30
Revolutions, engine, 122
Running-in new engine, 39

SEMI-automatic drip feed, 32
Sidecar, fitting, 41
Silencers, cleaning, 61
Sparking plug chart, 75
Speeds, equivalent, 121
Speeds of models, 30

Spitting back, 90
Starting-up, 38, 90

TECHNICAL data, 30
Tool kit, 46
Tuning, carburettor, 81
———, engine, 60
———, magneto, 69
Two-stroke, principles of, 3
Types of Villiers engines, 7

VILLIERS carburettor, 77
——— electric lighting systems, 92
——— fly-wheel magneto, 65

WORKING parts, 1
Worn cylinder, 59

PLEASE VISIT OUR WEBSITE - www.VelocePress.com - FOR AN UP-TO-DATE TITLE LISTING

AUTOBOOKS WORKSHOP MANUALS
ALFA ROMEO GIULIA 1300, 1600, 1750, 2000 1962-1978 WSM
BMW 1600 1966-1973 WSM
BMW 2500, 2800, 3.0 & 3.3 1968-1977 WSM
BMW 316, 320, 320i 1975-1977 WSM
BMW 518, 520, 520i 1973-1981 WSM
FIAT 1100, 1100D, 1100R & 1200 1957-1969 WSM
FIAT 124 1966-1974 WSM
FIAT 124 SPORT 1966-1975 WSM
FIAT 125 & 125 SPECIAL 1967-1973 WSM
FIAT 126, 126L, 126 DV, 126/650 & 126/650 DV 1972-1982 WSM
FIAT 127 SALOON, SPECIAL & SPORT, 900, 1050 1971-1981 WSM
FIAT 128 1969-1982 WSM
FIAT 1300, 1500 1961-1967 WSM
FIAT 131 MIRAFIORI 1975-1982 WSM
FIAT 132 1972-1982 WSM
FIAT 500 1957-1973 WSM
FIAT 600, 600D & MULTIPLA 1955-1969 WSM
FIAT 850 1964-1972 WSM
JAGUAR MK 1, 2 1955-1969 WSM
JAGUAR S TYPE, 420 1963-1968 WSM
JAGUAR XK 120, 140, 150 MK 7, 8, 9 1948-1961 WSM
LAND ROVER 1, 2 1948-1961 WSM
MERCEDES-BENZ 190 1959-1968 WSM
MERCEDES-BENZ 220/8 1968-1972 WSM
MERCEDES-BENZ 220B 1959-1965 WSM
MERCEDES-BENZ 230 1963-1968 WSM
MERCEDES-BENZ 250 1968-1972 WSM
MERCEDES-BENZ 280 1968-1972 WSM
MINI 1959-1980 WSM
MORRIS MINOR 1952-1971 WSM
PEUGEOT 404 1960-1975 WSM
PORSCHE 911 1964-1973 WSM
PORSCHE 911 1970-1977 WSM
RENAULT 16 1965-1979 WSM
RENAULT 8, 10, 1100 1962-1971 WSM
ROVER 3500, 3500S 1968-1976 WSM
SUNBEAM RAPIER, ALPINE 1955-1965 WSM
TRIUMPH SPITFIRE, GT6, VITESSE 1962-1968 WSM
TRIUMPH TR4, TR4A 1961-1967 WSM
VOLKSWAGEN BEETLE 1968-1977 WSM

VELOCEPRESS AUTOMOBILE BOOKS & MANUALS
ABARTH BUYERS GUIDE
AUSTIN-HEALEY 6-CYLINDER WSM
AUSTIN-HEALEY SPRITE & MG MIDGET 1958-1971 WSM
BMW 600 LIMOUSINE FACTORY WSM
BMW 600 LIMOUSINE OWNERS HAND BOOK & SERVICE MANUAL
BMW 2000 & 2002 1966-1976 WSM
BMW ISETTA FACTORY WSM
BOOK OF THE CARRERA PANAMERICANA - MEXICAN ROAD RACE
COMPLETE CATALOG OF JAPANESE MOTOR VEHICLES
CORVAIR 1960-1969 OWNERS WORKSHOP MANUAL
CORVETTE V8 1955-1962 OWNERS WORKSHOP MANUAL
DIALED IN - THE JAN OPPERMAN STORY
FERRARI 250/GT SERVICE AND MAINTENANCE
FERRARI 308 SERIES BUYER'S AND OWNER'S GUIDE
FERRARI BERLINETTA LUSSO
FERRARI BROCHURES AND SALES LITERATURE 1946-1967
FERRARI BROCHURES AND SALES LITERATURE 1968-1989
FERRARI GUIDE TO PERFORMANCE
FERRARI OPP, MAINTENANCE & SERVICE H/BOOKS 1948-1963
FERRARI OWNER'S HANDBOOK
FERRARI SERIAL NUMBERS PART I - ODD NUMBERS TO 21399
FERRARI SERIAL NUMBERS PART II - EVEN NUMBERS TO 1050
FERRARI SPYDER CALIFORNIA
FERRARI TUNING TIPS & MAINTENANCE TECHNIQUES
HENRY'S FABULOUS MODEL "A" FORD
HOW TO BUILD A FIBERGLASS CAR
HOW TO BUILD A RACING CAR
HOW TO RESTORE THE MODEL 'A' FORD
IF HEMINGWAY HAD WRITTEN A RACING NOVEL
JAGUAR E-TYPE 3.8 & 4.2 WSM
LE MANS 24 (THE BOOK THAT THE FILM WAS BASED ON)
MASERATI BROCHURES AND SALES LITERATURE
MASERATI OWNER'S HANDBOOK
METROPOLITAN FACTORY WSM
MGA & MGB OWNERS HANDBOOK & WSM
MG MIDGET TC, TD, TF & TF1500 WORKSHOP MANUAL
OBERT'S FIAT GUIDE
PERFORMANCE TUNING THE SUNBEAM TIGER
PORSCHE 356 1948-1965 WSM
PORSCHE 912 WSM
SOUPING THE VOLKSWAGEN
SOLEX CARBURETORS (EMPHASIS ON UK & EU AUTOMOBILES)
SU CARBURETORS (EMPHASIS ON UK AUTOMOBILES)
TRIUMPH TR2, TR3, TR4 1953-1965 WSM
TUNING FOR SPEED (P.E. IRVING)
VEDA ORR'S NEW REVISED HOT ROD PICTORIAL
VOLKSWAGEN TRANSPORTER, TRUCKS, STATION WAGONS WSM
VOLVO 1944-1968 ALL MODELS WSM
WEBER CARBURETORS (EMPHASIS ON ALFA & FIAT)

BROOKLANDS BOOKS & ROAD TEST PORTFOLIOS (RTP)
AC CARS 1904-2009
ALFA ROMEO 1920-1933 ROAD TEST PORTFOLIO
ALFA ROMEO 1934-1940 ROAD TEST PORTFOLIO
BRABHAM RALT HONDA THE RON TAURANAC STORY
BUGATTI TYPE 10 TO TYPE 40 ROAD TEST PORTFOLIO
BUGATTI TYPE 10 TO TYPE 251 ROAD TEST PORTFOLIO
BUGATTI TYPE 41 TO TYPE 55 ROAD TEST PORTFOLIO
BUGATTI TYPE 57 TO TYPE 251 ROAD TEST PORTFOLIO
DELAHAYE ROAD TEST PORTFOLIO
FERRARI ROAD CARS 1946-1956 ROAD TEST PORTFOLIO
FIAT 500 1936-1972 ROAD TEST PORTFOLIO
FIAT DINO ROAD TEST PORTFOLIO
HISPANO SUIZA ROAD TEST PORTFOLIO
HONDA ST1100/ST1300 PAN EUROPEAN 1990-2002 RTP
JAGUAR MK1 & MK2 ROAD TEST PORTFOLIO
LOTUS CORTINA ROAD TEST PORTFOLIO
MV AGUSTA F4 750 & 1000 1997-2007 ROAD TEST PORTFOLIO
TATRA CARS ROAD TEST PORTFOLIO

VELOCEPRESS MOTORCYCLE BOOKS & MANUALS
1930'S BRITISH MOTORCYCLE CARBS & ELEC COMPONENTS (BOOK OF)
1930'S BRITISH MOTORCYCLE GEARBOXES & CLUTCHES (BOOK OF)
AJS SINGLES & TWINS 250cc THRU 1000cc 1932-1948 (BOOK OF)
AJS SINGLES 1955-65 350cc & 500cc (BOOK OF)
AJS SINGLES 1945-60 350cc & 500cc MODELS 16 & 18 (BOOK OF)
ARIEL 1939-1960 4 STROKE SINGLES (BOOK OF)
ARIEL LEADER & ARROW 1958-1964 (BOOK OF)
ARIEL MOTORCYCLES 1933-1951 WSM
ARIEL PREWAR MODELS 1932-1939 (BOOK OF)
BMW M/CYCLES R26 R27 (1956-1967) FACTORY WSM
BMW M/CYCLES R50 R50S R60 R69S (1955-1969) FACTORY WSM
BSA BANTAM ALL MODELS FROM 1948 ONWARDS (BOOK OF)
BSA SINGLES & V-TWINS UP TO 1927 (BOOK OF)
BSA SINGLES & V-TWINS 1936-1939 (BOOK OF)
BSA SINGLES & V-TWINS 1936-1952 (BOOK OF)
BSA OHV & SV SINGLES 250-600cc 1945-1954 (BOOK OF)
BSA OHV & SV SINGLES - 250cc 1954-1970 (BOOK OF)
BSA OHV SINGLES 350 & 500cc 1955-1967 (BOOK OF)
BSA TWINS 1948-1962 (BOOK OF)
BSA TWINS 1962-1969 (SECOND BOOK OF)
CATALOG OF BRITISH MOTORCYCLES (1951 MODELS)
DOUGLAS PRE-WAR ALL MODELS 1929-1939 (BOOK OF)
DOUGLAS POST-WAR ALL MODELS 1948-1957 FACTORY WSM
DUCATI 160cc, 250cc & 350cc OHC MODELS FACTORY WSM
HONDA 50 ALL MODELS UP TO 1970 INC MONKEY & TRAIL (BOOK OF)
HONDA 90 ALL MODELS UP TO 1966 (BOOK OF)
HONDA MOTORCYCLES 125-150 TWINS C/CS/CB/CA WSM
HONDA MOTORCYCLES 250-305 TWINS C/CS/CB WSM
HONDA MOTORCYCLES C100 SUPER CUB WSM
HONDA MOTORCYCLES C110 SPORT CUB 1962-1969 WSM
HONDA TWINS & SINGLES 50cc THRU 305cc 1960-1966 (BOOK OF)
HONDA TWINS ALL MODELS 125cc THRU 450cc UP TO 1968 (BOOK OF)
INDIAN PONYBIKE, BOY RACER & PAPOOSE ILL PARTS LIST & SALES LIT
J.A.P. ENGINES 1927-1952 & MOTORCYCLES 1934-1952 (BOOK OF)
LAMBRETTA ALL 125 & 150cc MODELS 1947-1957 (BOOK OF)
LAMBRETTA LI & TV MODELS 1957-1970 (SECOND BOOK OF)
MATCHLESS 350 & 500cc SINGLES 1945-1956 (BOOK OF)
MATCHLESS 350 & 500cc SINGLES 1955-1966 (BOOK OF)
MOTORCYCLE ENGINEERING (P. E. Irving)
NORTON 1932-1947 (BOOK OF)
NORTON 1938-1956 (BOOK OF)
NORTON DOMINATOR TWINS 1955-1965 (BOOK OF)
NORTON MODELS 19, 50 & ES2 1955-1963 (BOOK OF)
NORTON MOTORCYCLES 1957-1970 FACTORY WSM
NORTON PREWAR MODELS 1932-1939 (BOOK OF)
NSU PRIMA ALL MODELS 1956-1964 (BOOK OF)
NSU QUICKLY ALL MODELS 1953-1963 (BOOK OF)
RALEIGH MOPEDS 1960-1969 (BOOK OF)
RALEIGH MOTORCYCLES 1919-1933 (BOOK OF)
ROYAL ENFIELD SINGLES & V TWINS 1934-1946 (BOOK OF)
ROYAL ENFIELD SINGLES & V TWINS 1937-1953 (BOOK OF)
ROYAL ENFIELD SINGLES 1946-1962 (BOOK OF)
ROYAL ENFIELD 736cc INTERCEPTOR FACTORY WSM
ROYAL ENFIELD 250cc & 350cc SINGLES 1958-1966 (SECOND BOOK OF)
RUDGE MOTORCYCLES 1933-1939 (BOOK OF)
SPEED AND HOW TO OBTAIN IT
SUNBEAM MOTORCYCLES 1928-1939 (BOOK OF)
SUNBEAM S7 & S8 1946-1957 (BOOK OF)
SUZUKI 50cc & 80cc UP TO 1966 (BOOK OF)
SUZUKI T10 1963-1967 FACTORY WSM
SUZUKI T20 & T200 1965-1969 FACTORY WSM
TRIUMPH PRE-WAR MOTORCYCLE 1935-1939 (BOOK OF)
TRIUMPH MOTORCYCLES 1935-1949 (BOOK OF)
TRIUMPH MOTORCYCLES 1937-1951 WSM
TRIUMPH MOTORCYCLES 1945-1955 FACTORY WSM
TRIUMPH TWINS 1945-1958 (BOOK OF)
TRIUMPH TWINS 1956-1969 (BOOK OF)
VELOCETTE ALL SINGLES & TWINS 1925-1970 (BOOK OF)
VESPA 1951-1961 (BOOK OF)
VESPA 125 & 150cc & GS MODELS 1955-1963 (SECOND BOOK OF)
VESPA 90, 125 & 150cc 1963-1972 (THIRD BOOK OF)
VESPA GS & SS 1955-1968 (BOOK OF)
VILLIERS ENGINE UP TO 1959 INC. 3 WHEELERS (BOOK OF)
VILLIERS ENGINE UP TO 1969 (BOOK OF)
VINCENT MOTORCYCLES 1935-1955 WSM

Please visit our website

www.VelocePress.com

for a complete up-to-date list of titles, descriptions, and secure online ordering using PayPal.

www.ingramcontent.com/pod-product-compliance
Lightning Source LLC
Chambersburg PA
CBHW070554170426
43201CB00012B/1844